Roots & Branches Series

A CURRICULUM OF THE SOUL

A CURRICULUM OF THE SOUL
VOLUME TWO

EDITED BY JOHN CLARKE AND ALBERT GLOVER

THE INSTITUTE OF FURTHER STUDIES
&
SPUYTEN DUYVIL
NEW YORK CITY

Trade edition published by Spuyten Duyvil Publishing
for the institute of further studies

CONTENTS

JAZZ PLAYING

the noises of our city
and laughter on the street
Sound in my ears
sounds of her city
autochthonal tones
or it's only a dream
the music shapes

these works are for
Don Cherry
John Clarke
Clifford Jordan
Tracy Hughes

Hail Sovereign Queen of Secrets

Venus Genetrix   or   Aphrodite

Venus—name for a planet
    She is here in Her   various aspects

Variegated Nature   in a yellow happy dress

She Who Clothes Her Selves Anew

this is the morning of initial appearances
  the flower of the first crocus
      prior to the unfolding
  the outward surface of the petals
displays   vivid white and purple
flashes   the white struck thru
with thin red veins.

    and today

our stars must glisten distinct with new fire
or be extending towards extinction

    All call the lovers of Ancient Days
      to dance the night away

AFTER THE CHANGES

To begin with a quotation from *Harvard Dictionary of Music* : Pitch—location of a musical sound in the tonal scale, proceeding from low to high . . . determination of pitch is by the frequency (number of vibrations of the sound.

Ornette writes: "There are some intervals that *carry* that *human* quality if you play them in the right pitch. I don't care how many intervals a person can play on an instrument; you can always reach into the human sound of a voice on your horn if you're actually hearing and trying to express the warmth of a human voice. I always write the melody line first because several different chords can fit the same melody line. In fact, I would prefer it if musicians would play my tunes with different changes as they take a new chorus so that there'd be all the more variety in the performance. If you feel the lines different one day, you can change the harmony accordingly."

"Rhythm patterns, should be more or less like natural breathing patterns. I would like the rhythm section to be as free as I'm trying to get, but very few players, rhythm or horns, can do this yet. Thelonious Monk can. He sometimes plays one note, and because he plays it in exactly the right pitch, he carries more music in it than if he had filled out the chord. Monk can also play different rhythm patterns, and a drummer I know, Edward Blackwell, is another musician who can play all kinds of time. If I don't set a pattern at a given moment, whoever has the dominant ear at that moment can take and do a thing that will release the direction from being what it always is into something else. And I believe in going along with him. The drummer can help determine direction too, because he can turn phrases around on a different beat, for example, thereby raising the freedom of my playing."

"Webster Armstrong used to tell me the musicians of his day would always talk about 'playing the bells.' They could hear free voices coming from the skies. I could just imagine voices which you couldn't see but could hear; they'd have to be angel voices because we see humans. In *Angel Voice*, if you listen closely to my part, it sounds like I'm playing the lead, and if you listen closely to Donald's, it sounds like he is."

Ornette Coleman

SOUND SHINES AND BIRD TALES

Thru the Palm Tree's green fronds
Sound returns old images
for I have turned to the old
ones for instruction.

No arrogance stems me,
tho kin wld have tamed
thee all.

Blood pulses
these ancient songs.

Flute pipes sing
to dreamless present
awake to heat
in blank screams
soaring
sound streams

I Praise thee Cherry
Man of Many Songs
yr birds whirl in empty skies,
blew easy thru the clear air,
turning in the breeze

Shake bells Clap hands All fall
Dream drum wood stroke Cymbal crash
new modes swirl old molds

Blow wind all away
walls crumble in the breeze
Lele-o   Ouayoh   Hay
Lele-o   Ouayoh

Many humans hearing the surfaces and content of music through referential mechanisms in the context of their culture register sensorial violation.

If they recognize delicacy of the player's articulations, sounds are suddenly experienced, the auditor is participant and light/heat gathers in Ascension.

· · ·

Narcissus says "I can love nothing now save bewitching water."

· · ·

Paul Valery writes: "By World I mean the whole complex of incidents, demands, compulsions, solicitations, of every kind and degree of urgency which overtakes the mind without offering it any inner illumination . . . so humans will attempt always with a plan to escape that World."

· · ·

"Plenty has made me poor."   Narcissus

"Jazz Playing"

The mouth gives
radiant outlet   Venus
to the winds
that draw the figures   Joy
moving over landscape
whirling vertically   Desire
from the belly
through throat   Sweet Fire
out   into the air
realizing
these areas
we inhabit
if only,
if only
we are there.

Marsyas, a follower of Cybele, innocently picked up the instrument that Athene discarded cursing any future players of this double stag-bone flute, when she saw the unflattering reflection of her distended face in the waters of a passing stream. The story is that the flute played the most incredibly far out and beautiful strains, inspired by the memory of Athene's music, as soon as Marsyas pressed the flute to his lips. He was traveling in Cybele's entourage throughout Phrygia and was drawing crowds thru his playing everywhere he went and the people dug it. But some fools got so excited they were shouting:

"Marsyas! You're the greatest!"

"Why Apollo ain't shit with that lyre of his."

"You got it Marsyas!" and Marsyas felt boss and if he was nervous abt the conditions of his playing, he could rest assured of the Goddess's protection as he was a loyal follower, and felt *good* playing, so he was happy to let the people rave on.

Well Apollo was ripshit—pissed off and affronted besides by the success of this low-life satyr and his loyalty to the old religion, so he called Marsyas and challenged him to a musical competition. What could Marsyas do? Since he'd picked up on that stag-bone flute at the river's edge, he'd been playing and playing—he'd have to go with the music and agree to the contest with Apollo; nothing else he could do now. So he consented and Apollo, being the challenger, empanelled the Muses as judges and set the terms—the winner could punish the loser however he wanted to. So lots of music—hours of song and the players played on. Everyone was delighted—the Muses and the people too, but in no way cld they select a winner, I mean by the time the music went down *that* was no longer the issue. Apollo wanted vengeance so he sang an impossible challenge:

"Play yr instrument upside down and sing as I am doing now."

Marsyas had to concede to Apollo's terms—he cldn't play a flute upside down and sing at the same time so those are the grounds he lost the contest on and his life and skin too, because after Apollo upended his lyre and played and sang praises to the honor of all the Olympians, the Muses had to give it to him and as soon as they did he got down to kicking ass and when he got tired of that he skinned Marsyas alive and nailed his skin to a pine tree and named the River that sourced near the spot Marsyas so that all the horn players and followers of the Goddess would remember. Robert Graves said the story does in fact "commemorate the Hellenic conquests of Phrygia and Arcadia and the consequent supercession in these regions of wind instruments by stringed ones, except among the peasantry."

Out of this World

When evening draws over this desolate town,
Strains of wild music where the rains stream down.

I see your face before I, Gita
In a Northern glance from Hertel Bridge
High in the eastward sorrowful walk
What spirit dreams put we on now?

Not sorrows to have done with home,
What turns me in the unknown deeps
To sing this song of the screaming trees?
What will you from the virgin sea?

This glittering waste in dawn's early light
Is drawing those lightless warriors home.
I move in the whispers of her dark heat.

Drawn in the tides of milk white foam
Thru the desolation of this Genesee Night
Her burning face shows the way back home.

John Coltrane's Letter to Don DeMicheal

June 2, 1962

Dear Don

Many thanks for sending Aaron Copland's fine book, *Music and Imagination*. I found it historically revealing and on the whole quite informative. However, I do not feel that all of his tenets are entirely essential or applicable to the 'jazz' musician. This book seems to be written more for the American classical or semi-classical composer who has the problem, as Copland sees it, of not finding himself an integral part of the musical community, or having difficulty in finding a positive philosophy or justification for his art. The 'jazz' musician (You can have this term along with several others that have been foisted upon us.) does not have this problem at all. We have absolutely no reason to worry about lack of positive and affirmative philosophy. It's built in us. The phrasing, the sound of the music attest this fact. We are naturally endowed with it. You can believe all of us would have perished long ago if this were not so. As to community, the whole face of the globe is our community. You see, it is really easy for us to create. We are born with this feeling that just comes out no matter what conditions exist. Otherwise, how could our founding fathers have produced this music in the first place when they surely found themselves (as many of us do today) existing in hostile communities where there was everything to fear and damn few to trust. Any music which could grow and propagate itself as our music has, must have a hell of an affirmative belief inherent in it. Any person who claims to doubt this, or claims to believe that the exponents of our music of freedom are not guided by this same entity, is either prejudiced, musically sterile, just plain stupid or scheming. Believe me, Don, we all know that this word which so many seem to fear today, 'Freedom' has a hell of a lot to do with this music. Anyway, I did find in Copland's book many fine points. For example: 'I cannot imagine an art work without implied convictions.'—Neither can I. I am sure that you and many others have enjoyed and garnered much of value from this well written book.

If I may, I would like to express a sincere hope that in the near future, a vigorous investigation of the materials presented in this book and others related will help cause an opening up of the ears that are still closed to the progressive music created by the independent thinking artist of today. When this is accomplished, I am certain that the owners of such ears will easily recognize the very vital and highly enjoyable qualities that exist in this music. I also feel that through such honest endeavor, the contributions of future creators will be more easily recognized, appreciated and enjoyed; particularly by the listener who may otherwise miss the point (intellectually, emotionally, sociologically, etc.) because of inhibitions, a lack of understanding, limited means of association or other reasons.

You know, Don, I was reading a book on the life of Van Gogh today, and I had to pause and think of that wonderful and persistent force—the creative urge. The creative urge was in this man who found himself so much at odds with the world he lived in, and in spite of all the adversity, frustrations, rejections and so forth—beautiful and living art came forth abundantly . . . if only he could be here today. Truth is indestructible. It seems history shows (and it's the same way today) that the innovator is more often than not met with some degree of condemnation; usually according to the degree of his departure from the prevailing modes of expression or what have you. Change is always so hard to accept. We also see that these innovators always seek to revitalize, extend and reconstruct the status quo in their given fields, wherever it is needed. Quite often they are the rejects, outcasts, sub-citizens, etc. of the very societies to which they bring so much sustenance. Often they are people who endure great personal tragedy in their lives. Whatever the case, whether accepted or rejected, rich or poor, they are forever guided by that great and eternal constant—the creative urge. Let us cherish it and give all praise to God. Thank you and best wishes to all.

Sincerely, John Coltrane

THE BICYCLE STORY

"Half the story has never been told."

After my father's death, his going away in 1950, nothing but loss. I was called Brownie in those days, alone, ancient and inconsolable. The conditions of wealth that he left me in only aggravated my sense of dispossession, made a mockery of the literal disinheritance. My mother, brother and I continued to live in the fashion declared by the appearance of an opulent materiality, as of the things/possessions and relationships of kin and persons involved in the various industrial activities concentric to the minings of iron ore and steel production that had enabled a vast resurgence of local wealth, in the twelve year period prior to his death, due to the promotion of the Second World War and adjacent economic adventures in remote (to U.S.A.) areas of the Earth, particularly ruinous to the inhabitants of Africa, Indo-China and South America in the years that followed the war. The war against fascism was fought and lost in Spain despite the fact that all of the Nations that supported Franco's policy of fascist rule, in most cases officially, were also the countries whose citizens formed volunteer units (in America the Abraham Lincoln Brigade celebrated on the Impulse recording of Charlie Haden's Liberation Music Orchestra) that traveled to Spain and fought in support of the legitimately elected Republican Forces. The war was fought and lost on that ground. Before America entered the European conflict thru an official declaration of war against Germany, traffic and trade with German industrialists, strong isolationist elements and a general, though for the most part unspoken, sympathy with fascist policy of strict enforcement of dictatorial rule in the suppression of citizens who didn't keep their place as of the maintenance of the industrial powers, allowed for a terrible vagueness that undercut finally whatever national conscience we may have once shared as a people. Once war was declared, the media of newspapers and magazines, radios and newsreels got behind the official decision, and within a week popular opinion was actively engaged in the various issues so that an almost unanimous feeling of warlike hatred against the Nazis emerged in a total enlistment of popular sentiment with the cause. I remember hearing how the powerful German Bunds throughout the Midwest dissolved within days, many of the members just going dumb, waiting to see how things were going to turn out. But this was the moment of realization for high level media personnel when it became completely obvious that, given any issue at all, the majority of citizens could be manipulated to practically any aspect of general opinion that the rulers thought was useful to their interests.

In the society that enveloped my mother and brother and me in Cleveland a material comfort was realized and somewhat idealized too in the mistaken belief that insulation was possible. Alexis de Tocqueville said it, maybe the first to run the mechanical analogy down on us: "A kind of virtuous materialism may ultimately be established in the world, which would not corrupt, but enervate the soul and noiselessly unbend its springs of action," so there's no need to describe that dreariness again. Novelists since Flaubert have been doing it for years delighting in the description or giving a form to falsehood and that's another story—"to map the monster that is yr own specificity." We lived in a large white house on North Park Boulevard, the route that followed the course of Doan Creek that sourced in Upper Shaker Lake and meandered as a brook to Lower Shaker Lake and falling from there into the pool where the main confluence continued in a series of rapids and water falls to an underground stream that emerged at the edge of the prairie in a lagoon to move from there in a gentle course to Lake Erie. In the Spring of 1951 after a particularly wet Winter, I used to go down to the pool below the Lake in the early morning and listen to the water fall on water and occasionally fish for the perch, bluegills and carp that appeared in mammoth schools that year. In those broodings by the pool amidst the weird night blooms of the place, I was often moved to go on my bicycle—one of those fat-tired fenderless Schwinns—along the paths through the ravine where Doan Creek flowed, sometimes checking out one of the three or four caves whose mouths opened in the face of the ravine; and made my way on the descent over two foothills that were forested at that time coming out of the Allegheny woods onto the Prairie / into the city and pedal over a mile on Liberty Boulevard to the Lagoon below University Circle and follow the footpaths that bordered the Creek for the eight mile ride thru the woods to Lake Erie 55 blocks East of the center of the city where the Terminal Tower stands. That day there was a wind off the Lake—the Lady sings The Winds of March that make my heart a dancer and the Poet asks "Does the world down all its rivers rave?"—and the water was much too cold for the briefest dip never mind a swim. The day was warm tho, and stretched out on one of the breakwater rocks [huge 9x9x9 cubes that were dumped by some official decision to retard erosion as some of the more powerful citizens of the community had built large, what they thought to be permanent, mansions near the shore of the Lake] and reflecting in Sunne's heat I dozed off hearing the waves, stormy storied Lake of shifting waters that swell in the blasts of wind. High waves beating on the Mysterious Gray Lake. No matter what anyone said or did in no way could I account for the death of my father—was he living someplace else detained as a prisoner or did he assume a different identity to begin again a new life. I couldn't speak with my younger brother about any of this—the words weren't there, yet I felt that we shared in this destiny—victims of a conspiracy of everyone—all the rest shared this secret of my father's whereabouts—to put us to the test—the singular trial of our young lives, and that if we made the right moves or the words came to me he would be back with us and all would be as it was: playing ball in the late June twilight, eternal Saturday morning hikes in the woods, the drives down to Mayfield Hill to watch the endless freight trains pass and all the wonderful adventures that evoked the aromas of his enormous presence forever. I knew this even before his death, when the dizzy spells came on and later at the hospital where they performed a brain operation making the cut, what my mother called the worry paths (lobotomy) and discovered the malignancy, and remembering then an earlier time of parthogenetic births attended by the grandest and most excruciating pains imaginable. I knew and could do nothing, and knew that if I didn't move or speak out the pressure would increase and he would finally die. At the time Dad went into the hospital, a few days later they moved him to Boston for the operation, I stopped growing, hung up in a physical limbo for two years, searching in growing despair three or four times a day for some sign of emerging hair around my groin, any slight change—even a pimple heralded momentarily the possibility of a voice change or the hair that my friends and classmates were so proud of or, even more dramatically, seemed to take for granted in the showers we took after a period of compulsory athletics at school every day and nothing. I mean nothing was happening at all. Even habits of physical care were neglected enough for impetigo to get started and flourish causing exotic blotchy eruptions to appear around my cheeks and mouth and clumps of hair to fall out. A few months before this day I'm remembering, I had been hospitalized for what was diagnosed as osteo-malitis after falling down the back stairs of the house when my left leg became suddenly and unaccountably paralyzed. Anyway it seems this course of self-neglect began to turn when I heard the family doctor and my mother speaking of a projected series of complicated operations involving what I understood to be bone transplants and extensive scraping at the marrow of my thigh bone, I began to respond to the sulfa drugs and regain some feeling in my leg. I don't know for sure, but I remember periods of the most wonderful feelings of well being and the initial dreams of traversal through extra-terrestrial realms adjacent to Earth space so it's likely that I was experiencing the benign effects of traditional medicines for the first time coincident with the other experiences from the sulfa. Penicillin was not in widespread use at the time and the more powerful antibiotics were only being used experimentally. This March afternoon on the rocks, still hung up in an inarticulate agony but with that paralysis of my leg well behind me, only suffering a slight itching pain on the dampest days, I was beginning to get about some, but this was as far away from home as I'd been since Dad died and I thought about that and pedaling back up Cedar Hill and maybe stopping for a milkshake on the way home, yes I had a quarter, so I started home with the slow awareness of coming awake—that early Spring feeling of lazing around easy and yr blood warms anyway. An unlooked for optimism coming on despite any attempts to continue brooding and dwell on my father's absence. After setting out only those marginal impressions peripheral to feeling, spring sap rising new in the bough darkens the bark of the elm trees, pine, sumac, ash and maple returning by the same route along Liberty Boulevard and just before the 79th Street turnoff a white Cadillac cuts in real close and I determine to make the turn and pedal south on 79th Street to Carnegie or Cedar and go home by way of Cedar Hill. Well I must have traveled four miles on 79th Street as in a dream when you go from one place to another passing all intervening space in an instant—one place / the image of the place then the next and no conscious traversal of the space—you are simply there and I was there making that turn at 79th Street going west on Euclid Avenue, a lot of auto traffic and not so many people on the sidewalk so I jumped the curb and slowed down wondering how I got across the intervening four miles and hadn't traveled more than 20 yards when I heard the most incredible sounds . . . I came alive.

I have never been able to describe the music I heard that Sunday afternoon. Someone had mounted one of those cone speakers over the door of Lindsy's Sky Bar and the music was pouring out. (Anyone reading this who has grown up with the questionable advantages of stereo and various technological advances in the realm of sound fidelity cannot imagine the quality of that sound.) In that single instant of the initial hearing I knew that nothing else mattered. It wasn't very complicated. This music was in the world and I had a life to live. What someone called "the ancient bond of consanguinity, real or imagined" was evoked. I was aware of my deep kinship with the players of the music before I knew who they were—the community was there. I stood straddling the boy bar of the bike for the better part of an hour listening to the songs. A space was being given, not in any architectural sense, as the ground was changing in the wake of new pieces, traces of the ancient songs of seashore and grassland savannah—the music of primordial man and all the intervening history experienced in a turn of phrasing, the agony of what I had assumed to be a private experience of loss articulated publicly. The sound of the horn in an unimaginable array of textural declarations grew distinct in signature from the other players. I saw through the open door the man who stood up crouched over his horn playing *Confirmation*, a song learned from the music of many birds and many waters.

Comin down off the bluff, Cleveland Heights, the western edge of the foothills of the Alleghenies, into the City where the music was on Cedar Avenue. The Ebony Lounge, Jack's Musical Bar, and the Corner Tavern; south on Woodland to Gleason's Musical Bar—hearin Ray Charles and his band with Fathead, Marcus Belgrave, Betty Carter and Blackwell for the first time—*Hallelujah I Love Her So*—and next door, to the <u>Chatterbox</u> (since dynamited by the guineas) where first time out I met some Bahamians, who had just come to Cleveland, jamming Calypso Drums finding out how high the music was in the cold North. I heard Lady Day sing in the Chatterbox and two years later The Queen came to town with Wynton.

Further south on Woodland toward the Terminal Tower and near the old Farmer's Market to the Club Congo—all the people drinking "house beer" out of unlabeled bottles—Jacktown playin a four and a half foot bass drum, the Lamia on the skin undulating whomp to his foot mallet pedal four beats to the bar, hi hat cymbals crackin on the second and fourth and Joe Alexander pickin up now.

Lamentation Over the Destruction of Cleveland

Dameron's Hut   The Ebony Lounge

Club Congo
                    Corner Tavern
Cafe Tiajuana   Lindsy's Sky Bar

Loop Lounge   Cedar Gardens

Gay Cross   /for After Hours/   Maceo's

   the Rose Room of the Majestic Hotel

   for Blue Monday . . .   Gleason's Musical Bar

The Cellar on Woodland Avenue

   and the Subway Club in the basement of the Hotel Carnegie

and the others: Modern Jazz Room

originally called The Cotton Club

          Chatterbox

          Leo's Casino on Central Avenue

          Hanna Lounge

and later going East on Euclid Avenue

          101 Club

          Algiers

          and Finally the Jazz Temple at the edge of the Prairie

"THE DIVINE NAMES MANIFEST IN THE PHENOMENAL VEIL"

"The story of jazz is a long list of great names . . ."

John Coltrane, McCoy Tyner, Elvin Jones, Jimmy Garrison, Philly Joe Jones, Joe Alexander, Tad Dameron, Clifford Brown, Max Roach, Sonny Clark, the Turrentine brothers—Stanley and Tommy, Bill Hardman, Ernie Shepard, Bill Gidney, Bunns, Gus Rosario, Jacktown, Spencer Thompson, Bob Cunningham, Tony Haynes, Charles Crosby, Roland Kirk, Abdul, Jack Hill, Herb Schindler, John Clarke, Bobby Castle, Weasel Parker, Lawrence Jackson, Fats Heard, Sonny Rollins, Walter Davis Jr., Ahmad Jamal, Vernal Fournier, Frank Gant, Paul Quinichette, Sir Charles Thompson, Sonny Stitt, Paul Chambers, Wynton Kelly, Dizzy Gillespie, Ernie Henry, Benny Golson, Billy Mitchell, Al Gray, Melba Liston, Talib Daawood, E. V. Perry, Bama Warwick, Lee Morgan, Paul West, Charlie Persip, Dinah Washington, Jimmy Cobb, Sarah Vaughn, Roy Haynes, Henry Grimes, Don Cherry, Billy Higgins, Charlie Haden, Ornette Coleman, Dewey Redman, Ed Blackwell, Dennis and Huss Charles, Art Blakey, Kenny Dorham, Hank Mobley, Horace Silver, Doug Watkins, Donald Byrd, Jackie McClean, Spanky de Brest, Bobby Timmons, Wayne Shorter, Freddie Hubbard, Jymie Merritt, Curtis Fuller, Cedar Walton, Sam Jones, Cannonball and Nat Adderley, Ray Brown, Milt Jackson, Percy Heath, Jimmy Heath, Albert Heath, Mtume, Azar Lawrence, John Stubbenfield, Jean Carns, Billy Hart–Jabali, Ndugu, Buster Williams—Mchezaji, Leroy Jenkins, Reggie Workman, Sonelius Smith, Joe Lee Wilson, Richard Williams, Eddie Preston, Teddy Edwards, Harold Land, Bobby Hutcherson, Stanley Cowell, Bill Lee, Ben Webster, Jimmy Blanton, Sonny Greer, Bubber Miley, Joe "Tricky Sam" Nanton, Barney Bigard, Harry Carney, Otto "Tubby" Hardwick, Juan Tizol, Lawrence Brown, Arthur Whetsol, Cootie Williams, Ray Nance, Cat Anderson, Duke Ellington, Johnny Hodges, Dexter Gordon, Duke Jordan, Clifford Jordan,

Charles Mingus, Charles Parker, Thelonius Sphere Monk, Kenny Clarke, Bud Powell, Oscar Pettiford, Clark Terry, Sahib Shihab, G. T. Hogan, Dizzy Reece, Harold McNair, George Symonette, Blind Blake, Freddie Cummings, Roy Burrows, Julian Priester, Johnny Coles, Booker Ervin, Danny Richmond, Jackie Byard, Eric Dolphy, Richard Davis, J. C. Moses, Wilbur Ware, Lester Young, Jessie Drake, Count Basie, Walter Page, Freddie Green, Jo Jones, Frank Foster, Eddie "Lockjaw" Davis, Gene Ammons, Johnny Griffin, Billie Holiday, Buck Clayton, Harry Edison, Don Byas, Teddy Wilson, Roy Eldridge, Coleman Hawkins, Barry Harris, Lonnie Hilyar, Charles McPherson, Lonnie Liston Smith, Dave Hubbard, Cecil McBee, Lawrence Killian, Pharoah Sanders, Sirone, Leon Tomas, Nat Bettis, Howard Johnson, Sonny Sherrock, Majeed Shabaz, Chief Bey, Randy Weston, Azzedin Weston, Ray Copeland, Julius Watkins, Fats Navarro, Miles Davis, Red Garland, Herbie Hancock, Tony Williams, Paul Weeden, Billy James, Don Patterson, Big Jay McNeely, Bull Moose Jackson, Lynn Hope, Willis "Gator-Tail" Jackson, Tab Smith, Earl Bostic, Louis Armstrong, Sidney Bechet, Earl Hines, Bud Johnson, Milt Hinton, Lyle Atkinson, Betty Carter, Danny Nixon, Al Harewood, Sun Ra, John Gilmore, Pat Patrick, Marshall Allen, Ali Hassan, Clifford Jarvis, Charles Davis, Larry Ridley, Ronny Boikins, Lex Humphries, Gary Peacock, Sonny Murray, Albert Ayler, Donald Ayler, Frank Wright, J.J. Johnson, Tommy Flanagan, Arthur Taylor, Cecil Taylor, Woody Shaw, Rene McLean, Ronnie Mathews, Stafford James, Louis Hayes, Sonny Fortune, Charles Sullivan, Kenny Baron, Wayne Dockery, Chip Lyle, Richie Pablo Landrum, Angel Allende, Bobby Clark, Charlie La Chapelle, David Murray, Bobo Shaw, Marion Brown, Sonny Brown, Julius Hemphill, Abdul Wadud, Olu Dara, Grachan Moncur III, Roswell Rudd, Hod O'Brien, Sheila Jordan, BuBu Monk, Don Pullen, George Adams, Dollar Brand, Art Tatum and so many others . . .

<u>Wildness Knows Practice ! ! Wildness Knows
neither Prudence nor Restraint</u>

Lustral Water

Ocean's Rivers

through the currents   the wall is there

Agony

we live in

.   .   .

the ship fashioned in the

new modes

out of wood

We who live in Sea   swimming
  in Water

the Sea Fans Wave

Sing Praise to Sea Mare   Coral   Lady

"Call was very important in that kind of music. Today the music has grown
up and become quite scholastic, but this was *au natural*, close to the primi-
tive, where people send messages in what they play, calling somebody, or
making facts or emotions known. Painting a picture, or having a story to
go with what you were going to play was of vital importance in those days.
The audience didn't know anything about it, but the cats in the band did."

Duke Ellington

storm winds   reading the waters

undersea earth quakes   riding the waves

Remember the moves
"forget the changes"

Old Moods   New Modes   <u>Keep True</u>
   to the dreams   of thy youth
     under sail   beneath the wind

wooden ship moves
        through the oceans
    that englobe the Earth
        from Caucasus Park
     to Plum Island
      to Negril

Feeling evening stillness
sumac torches moving
in the faintest breeze.
The Second Day of Harvest
Lodi Apples green
and fat, the thick stems
turned from the branch
in heavy snaps
and the humidity
so thick in the air
only the salt of the sea
distinguishes
immersions changes

Water children wonder
how many dark powers
claim us for their own
in the deeps of the sea

Tongue of Plum Island
in the River's mouth

the song of our brother
dusky demon of the shore,
yr words up
from the waves walking South
on the flat back of the beast
so High
   the low waves
lisping our destinies

wake to the waves
on the beach
from Negril
to Plum Island
The Song is You
whoever
you are

                    July 8, 9, 10, 1976

Turn A Round

   "How the hills
    spirit water"

How the hills rise
to my eyes raised
from the leaves
where the perfectly
red apple rests
hips enfolded in
the highest crotch
of this tree.
     Thursday, August 19, 1976

"Go Up In The Hills"

I hear speaking in the trees
limbs bending to winds
leaves waving in the breeze
ripe fruit shining how many
apples in the orchard leaves
singing in the darkness ripe
in bunches strung on the suckers
the songs are sung and I'm
hung in the air only my feet
on the rungs, my hands pick
the fruit from her hair.

<u>Monday Morning Labor Day: 11:05AM</u>

Waiting for her to arrive is waking up into the dream. Since I saw her in December, the play, the long night of the poem, waking up on the beach in Jamaica, the summer on the Plum Island Beach—days and nights when Holly was here from New York. Returning to work at the Orchard in late July.

<u>Saturday September 18, 1976</u>

In the fair orchard,
full of trees with fruit
the Pickers Rage,
bottoming out into
the dark places
filled at their appearance
with unmannerly energies.

We pick in the early morning
hours, the fruit shadowed
in the leaves and branches
wet in the night dew,
and as the skin
of the fruit warms to
rays, our clothes grow
heavy with the sweat
and dew from leaves.

Hands independent from
each other now left
and right wind thru
branches turning the fruit
stem against spur
to the weakest place of
connection where snap
happens apple palmed
and rolled to hand's heel

and the hand moves
to the next and always
first apple . . .

In our speech we are struggling to be here against the forces of vertigo—
that fusion which drains everything towards the depths. We give voice and
actualize in story multitudinous forms and shapes thru embryonic images
that are recognized if life moves there. What is truly new often appears
complex and difficult, to the hearer whose unclear perceptions distort the
very nature of the creation. And then the nervous reception of these figures
at the instant of their issue confuses their life and movement in the universe
so the whole suffers.

        River

         When the αιών of the body

the liquid

    issues in new life

    the life giving stream

  flowing to fullness

    the river brings

      drinking water

  washing the stones

    the water

  springs from

Don't Sit Under the Apple Tree
                    after Coleman Hawkins

no ladder points towards "Heaven" for me
glad for wooden rungs to the top of this tree

        High
        Inspired I see
        yr face be
        for me

        gazing into the West
        Sunne's descent burns my eyes
        and beckons I and I and
        I again to follow my feet
        burning to meet
        on the far side of the Falls.

DANCE
AS INDIVIDUAL BODY-POWER

I have got the holy ghost and I dance.

I believe in the sanctified people.

MAHALIA JACKSON
1911–1972

TO PHOEBE

Well, you know,

you know we wanta get down.

We wanta get down and say

we got to get down and say

we got to get up out of bed in the middle of the night
and the moon's just coming up and there's a copper and
kettle color floating on the mountains,
    and a jay misplaced, shrieks, then
Order.
                Flesh always,

Flesh always, flesh always

ROLLING TOWARD THE WALL

I often find myself eliminated
staring out of my cell in a septic tank
of newspaper images at great big super sculptures
big marble men striding across the forest
talking excitedly non-stop, taking twenty-mile strides
toward a head with a hole in it. I look
at a book:

"Relief From Today's Pressures"

—How ?

The chanting in Tibet has not stopped !
Only the soup kitchen has closed, and the Salvation Army has gone home
a drunken mummy.

—with Michael Brownstein

Doctors get sick
Pimps don't wink
Angels don't arrive in the nick of time &
they're not gonna stop Lew if he wants to go
kill himself in the woods and they know
                                    and they go
    away anyway
                    in the air
                            with a head full of snow
and watch the late show
the late show

Jim and Tandy Brodey stepping down from a bus in front of King-Of-The-Sea

THE AGE OR AEON

An overcast autumn day wrapping landscape and figures in a silver-grey melancholy inspired this picture. The artist strikes a noble chord of sadness in nature, by whose charm no one can fail to be drawn. No bright or garish color sounds a disturbing note. It is true we hear the shining waiters, but only as a throbbing bass register on which the yellows, blues, and violets weave their sad, balding melancholies. They do this in a framework formed by the branches and the undergrowth along the river bank, a framework of horizontals and verticals, one of which is the bridge which gives the picture its name. The figure has no more life than the masts of a boat, all but one of which have furled their sails. The effect, though, is not quite benumbing. Rather so rhythmic is its smooth equilibrium that it was not hard for later painters to adore Khonsu anonymously, after this example of bright liaison.

(OCEAN)

Everything revolves around your belly !

TURNER

A cascade of dreams and susses

Loganberry marmalade

covered with dirt I am cowed and grounded

and covered with care   I grow afraid of the shadow &

Man, I was one.

I grow sleepy and I rage:

Oh Martyr's beautiful daughter

sliding down the banister

to join me

I feel the blue fangs of your father

inside of me and silently wise

TO ANNE

There's nothing on earth

that's the matter with death

    I see your face

engaged and aging

We dance together

by the light of the moon

PLAYA DE PRIMAVERALES, GUAYMAS

Cries and rumblings in the shaky hours before dawn
Wake us. Moon gone. Cold gone. Sandpipers
criss-cross the tidal pools below soft Venus light
on your breast most purest womanly form revealed
through a loose boy's shirt in a sleeping bag I roll toward
to heat up before daylight sun blasts and man stands alone with just
fifty-five centavos for an orange crush grande and no coy,
sexual, pacific darkness. I love you ! I marry you ! Speech good !

The less baggage you carry the easier it is to go.

•

"Dance" as individual body-power. Anti-Gravity. In "weightlessness" (one-sixth gravity) the scope of movements increases as control over them diminishes.

•

Peggy Mosley knows how to do <u>the</u> <u>breakdown</u>. Do we have a verb for <u>connâitre</u>?

•

The Origin of the Shakers. (Marvin Gaye's "What's Going On")

•

Malo, Ala.

•

Thank you brother Glenn. In revolution one wins
and one dies. Strike down the marijuana laws. Feed
honkies to the chickens ! (whew)

•

Net-dances of the biosferic pre-date stone tools.

•

Now the dada painters too, live in the world of silence.

•

Good-by to a million years bicycling, circling off now to Jupiter on a plak.

•

Buddy Holly was the father of The Wild Boys. The Wild Boys were the fathers of men.

•

Paul Valery = the Beachboys

—with Tom Clark.

God

                            No responsibilities

I say the eye proceeds command
so I built you this bower
but the scare crow fell over   Melted Bluejay
in the northwest rain. The bower held,
the peas are fine. Blue sky,   chastened by fire
grey seas, & steam
rises off the rye grass
following the clouds south, returning.   Gravity

                             The Grave

OUT OF SIGHT OF LAND

   And the sea buzzing and I'm spinning like an ant at sea

All fired with The Fear of Destiny and tilth . . .

                    a pair of quail in the yard, briefly

PHOEBE

Emol

Emul

     a watch fob

     a pink feather duster

     a key

     a handbook of keys, prophylaxis

tilting the small

     blue

        dithyramb

     seapeople,

          Bolinas

     2 (two) ★ ★

       Air

       Space

       The Poetry Room

       Where I Hang My Hat

then draw and color in a background scene
consisting of a mountain range with the sun and the shadows
as they would appear on a summer mid-afternoon
(cloudless sky)

signed the contract today

OCEAN

Be fertile as I wish to be fertile

In the magic loaves of men.

RAW HONEY

Bumble bees ! Don't worry about the bumble bees,
they won't sting the baby

& even if they do he's only gonna swell up briefly.

But Phoebe

  says No.

The beehive above the porch has got to go.

Well fuck it.

If I could parrot the bumble bee
   I'd be the lost ecology,
  famous Al Lurch
 of World Environment
    stepping through the door of the Future Studies Center &
recoiling
  told me:

   "Even in our experimental manure shed we have no flies. None !
    We have discovered a cycle—
   Eight different insects—
     that when placed inside a prepared boxcar
    reach a perfect balance—i.e.

No more fruit flies. This way

We have control."

2.

I guess I'm sloppy.
In fact, I know I'm sloppy.

But the two bees working on the sugar in the dregs of
my coffee cup
Let me sing.

Give me song to sing. Give me focus and legend,

and following their whirr outside I see unchallenged gold

in the waters of Bolinas Bay

and the slight south wind surrounding

their departure brings me morning's second whiff of coffee

followed closely by your palm on my cheek and your voice

aching softly asks would I like a piece of fresh baked bread and butter ?

With a little honey ?

FIRST BANANA

Phoebe dips a curved blue spoon into
the soft mouth of the Ocean, then
retrieves it from the lips of Ocean Lee, the baby
frowns, he grins!   He can dig it !

BOSTON'S ANGEL

Many cross x's affirm the vows
you took the day Charles Olson
walked away across Boston Common
with your woman in tow. For you
saw his needs flamed higher in her eyes
and after three centuries of want
you would not be fulfilled by a woman
so now know better. Though you put up
storm shelters on the walls of your father's
residential hotel at sundown when
the smoke rises and once again, the nigger
burns the town, I am assured by
the throb in my pocket that your hunger
will go unavenged, assuaged only by the
faculty death wish, that the Nile rises high in the
mountains where shepherds chase gulls toward Madonna
down cataracts and the high rise sprays milk
across cool terra-cotta in the Nubian music dream.

LUXOR

Herd fever,
as your face
        incredibly washes away
a statue of an egg emerges
from the Honey Goddess

At last, my moniker ! No,
it is the coo of a witch I hear
tugging at my lame arrears
        and floods and puke also
    and dreams
        executed by the dread other
Half dead.
Proof, I said.

It is half life
 There is honey in your harmony
        There is harm here somewhere
    Foolproof, you said the

Lame blooms, you vex
She swore fever, not
        the serene.

  The natural history
        is of course severe
 the flies are drifting
out of the colossus

to echo in the
craving for beer. Hunters
of sheep, discursive
            sleep
          the sleep of
  monstrous flies

whose disastrous shadows
      enfold the
              tongue
and jar the dew these
        Pharaohs drowned
            their zeal in,

    In the haze zooms
a recollection
my kinship
my flower
burning in you
as some guiding
            principle sends my
penis sliding up your butt
in the chapel of Blue Amun.

Mother Dame, I was partied by some weird ones this afternoon

and I treated them to deference, the same as I've often treated you.

When the sea came off the lagoon through the alders it was totally your flame.

___WING___

Expectorant is spit, right ?

Everytime I find something beautiful

I fuck it up

and bring it home to you.

I stand tall like my father
did at his great hour,
noon

WING

I saw 10,000 talking and they were planning on
meeting each other at noon in the history booth
down at the World's Fair.

      "Bostock"—   "Present"

      Sharon   —   Here

      Banana   —   Well it's hard

to envision the scope unanimous & it's hard
to bring the world to bear on its own senses.
Not a one of us lives without the constant retreat
of the eye in the pellets of light. I told Bill last Monday night
that it's time to fold the game away and put away the cards.
Put it all away with play,
and the lights in her eyes were shining deep down in the bottom of the bay
and strange animals were striding up out of the swamp; babies,
bearing the flower that man-hood's song opens inwards
rigorous firm and proud

NAM AMIDA BUTSU

Let me pass the peas at dinner

let me pick you up and pack you off to sleep

"the obverse of this future studies trip"

is the route of the inward pelican

& I believe in the spinal whirls

as the moon comes up

the depth of glee

it comes !

Yellow Leader

in the window panes

obtained

in time: Music by Lou Reed

—with Ted Berrigan

Finished tacking down the tar-paper roof and sealed it.

      Stacked up

the hay and the feed mash, and the seed

      together in a warm corner, piled the tools and the loose hay,

hung the door.

Beat the rains

And I run
just like the wind will
after the windmill
for your love

EGYPTIAN HIEROGLYPHS

20,000 A.D.

The Council of Eye Forms
a liberal, nay even radical body of
intergalactic deities

composed itself upon various mutually agreeable
dimensions—namely those dimensions denigrated
by some, not in the Council of course, as "useless
Thrill-dimensions"—but nonetheless, a suitable
series of dimensions for communication among the
members of the Council of Eye Forms,

the purpose of the meeting being a general tactical
discussion of the aeon-long "Apopis problem"—
now that Apopis had apparently been caused to crumble
into desuetude in the so-called

        14th-emanation dungeon
        of gutted phantoms.

In the texts
Apopis was always stun-stomped
but like
an angry maniac
or stare-at-me! psychopath
        strode / slithered
        forth forever & a day
        to the boos and hisses
        of th' blobs
        of conscious molecules.

1) execration

2) sympathetic magic
          were the traditional scams

      by which the priests
      paralyzed Snake

        at the "critical moment"

      when Snake

        was going to

chew the lightnings and erg-sprays
off the sun
like a flower

          to leave
          a vermiform sky-ice
          scene for

          the apparent purpose of
          the self of him
          to writhe in worship
          of himself as the Total.

With a corona of fabricated TV broadcasts
a long eel in coils
of knife-stabbed red waves
upon the nadir of encroachment,

what a struggle, in lives & gore & misery
it was

    to tap those blades
          into the rolling back
                of Apopis.

Accordingly, and be it remembered that this just
a tale, The Council
held Snake 'neath the fierce administration of
          an N-dimensional
             milky way-μολυ

               or trance-moly.

Silence reigned where shrieks were once the revenue.
Drops could be heard
in the golden chalice

      it was so silent
      upon the belly of the
      All.

But
the august sere angst-heads

debated
far too far into the "night"

the question of Apopis

e'en with the knowledge of so many trillions of ex-cons
(Council term: expansion/contraction of the Big)
when Worm rode berserk—

but now! lay stunned
within his current form of
175,000 miles of starshine snakegrease.

    Think upon it earthling:
    to rid the star-pelt all
    of gore-gobble.

    For a' that and a' that
    the good Council
    shed tears

        o'er the death-hacked Apopis

though Apopis
    spat hate
        & crests of destruction

"Each morn
he tried to bushwhack
the sun

       arising in
       the arms
       of perfect love!"—railed

           the prosecutor
           Eye Form

But eve-time
found the hate worm—
knives in his back jangle / jiggling

      ready to
     suck the yummy fires
       of

And pray to know why the Council of Eye Forms
did hesitate to snuff forever
vengeful, violent, remorseless

street-punk
  on the avenues
     of the Universal Hole?

"Dost 'ou *really* really pine for Apep
be a lawless field-fluid of crazed gravity?"—
sang a languid Form nicknamed The Coma in
many a set of dimensions.

And many shuddered indeed at such a "thought."

Meanwhile the trance-moly waned.
And pity raised up the child of pity,
manumission.

      Turgid, then slowly warping
      then faster faster faster

         Apopis rolled, coil 'pon coil,

        out of the dungeon
      shrieked and cackled
      farting clouds of revenge,

spitting a promise of merry pain-mass
    to all the beastie bands of molecules

    grew out of the nature of mad Sky
      to stare and dare and be aware
        beloved 'pon beloved.

I want

to be purified

in the

she sang

THE SINGER

The blind harp-strummer
sat before the vizir's banquet
singing of shrieks and shrieks
and thoughts of shrieks and symbol shrieks
and new shrieks bouncing surly
down upon the faded shrieks of faded pain

"Hang garlands on the neck of your wife
and garlands on her arms,

and listen overhead"—sang the blind Egyptian harper
"and listen underfoot
and sing when there is silence
and sing when there is safety
and sing sing sing"

    While 4600 years later
    there was once a singer
    and a writer of songs
    who worked in a bar far off
    near Blabtos, Georgia

    The week was up and the singer walked
    into the office of the club
    collecting he hoped the rest of his
    pay

which had to be given him
all in cash
according to the terms of his contract
with the club

The owner looked askance
at the tired grimy person of tunes, he
snorted down from his nose just as
he hooted smoke from his mouth
and the grey boiled downward, disappeared

 The sheriff's been
 looking at the wheels
 of your van and they
 don't look none too safe

 Besides you sing
 ugly, little man
 your band belongs
 in a high school basement

 We reckon a hundred dollars
 and a free trip out of town
 ought to do you right good.

But you owe me 300 dollars!
Sweat was breaking out upon his long
black sideburns

& his eyes were wide with piss-off
sweat too spread over his blue satin shirt
wherever there was hair beneath

And the band's got to get their pay
Mr. Parsons!

    No mind to me
    son, he replied
    I don't give no frig
    for those tub thumps
    call themselves a band

    But those hundreds of folk
    who came! What about
    them? Hunh! My customers
    come for to guzzle
    boy, don' forget it
    guzzle! guzzle!
    Now take this hundred
    and get   and don't
    go howling to my cousin
    over at the union
    neither.

Sheriff! He's in here
givin' me some lip.
And watch your badmouthing me
hear?

I ain't going out of here
till you 'fill the terms
of my contract. He pulled
the wadded wet-with-sweat document
out of his back pocket
unfolded it & held it
up to the light—I'll have to sue

Give me that! the owner snarled
and grabbed it out of his hand
tore it shreds

The singer
knocked the owner down
locked him
shirt pulled up his back
saw the white kidney—
twinge of evil, singer couldn't
stop his hand   hack the
fatty mountain—aiee! the
head of the owner flipped back and forth
lips slobber pain.
Help! Murder . . . kidneys! Sheriff!

The sheriff banged open the
door, door-edge thudded
the singer's side
He pulled them apart   then clubbed
the singer with the gun-butt
thomp! thomp! Goddamn greasy

little pretender. Why don't you
get a haircut? I heard you, off-color songs
mixed up w/ church songs. You got
no right to put on an act like that.
Mr. Parsons's right to pay you what
you deserve.

    Now you get on out of here
    in that van of illegality
    you call a home—

And the sheriff
pushed him
staggering for balance out of
the club, past the sweepers bent
in the sawdust, into the
alley.

With sounds of ptuh! ptuh!
he sputtered the blood from his lips
and started the engine
then let the steel guitar player drive
when he got the urge to sing
and crawled into the back of the van
where he pulled a guitar off the wall
and sang with throbbing mouth of cuts
almost till dawn
when the van pulled up at
a motel near the Tennessee border.

AB-MER

Hathor's farm and school of every art
had a fine broad lake
square as perfection
cornered by the finest Acacia trees
the breasts of Isis
hung from the branches

The gardens and orchards of Hathor's House of Life
moiled with abundance, the flocks
of animals grew like the seed of Ptah
under the urging of Hathor

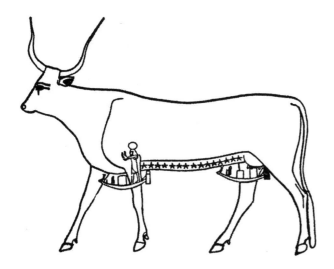

How many hundred-weights of honey
lay stored within the House of Hathor,
Countless, the bees of Hathor buzzed within the long reed hives
and poets writing lyrics walked blossom'd acres

So what if the quarter-mile wall
around the House of Hathor was rather in need of repair?
What midget from the
robber camps in the marshes
would climb up over to steal?
What jewels were there to
steal from the House of Hathor?
What thief would want
long poems on parchment?
What could he get for that? since
Limited Signed Editions were 1000's of years away.

What was the price of sketches
on old wine casks?
No robber after gold
or red stones would bother
when the graves of the desert
held tons of wealth.

Soldiers patrolling the wasteland temples of wealthy dead
with long-snouted dogs on leash
whispered how displeased the vizir's agents were
with Hathor's Rebel House of Life.

By the standards of the time, 1985 B.C.
in the beginning of the first of the
Middle Kingdom dynasties, it was a small House of Life,
but self-sufficient,
collecting to its walls the finest painters, dancers,
singers, poets, musicians, stone workers, wine makers

and tasters of the above, rebels all, full of energy
and full of love of Hathor and Hathor's whispered 'joinder to Ra:
"Part thy robes, O Ra, and we shall conjoin."

    Ready were the artists of Hathor to fill the valley Nile
    with beatnik potsherds, Hathor lore, papyri drawn with visions
    never seen beneath the deity-clogged skies of overarching Nut.

    Nothing sang as sweet
    as Hathor's singers
    No one could raise the skin
    and the scatter-dance of love
    so far into the heights
    as Hathor's singers

What a school of singers was the House of Hathor

    None could draw with
    such consummate skill
        as the draughtsmen of Hathor
    No one could raise such thundering anger
    from petty clerks in the civil government
        as the draughtsmen of Hathor

    and the poets raised up such a complete complex
    of derision and anger

    "Put trivia upon the basalt blocks. It's
    better than lists of captive slaves" was sort
    of the motto of the House

which caused the court-creeps to rail with anger, urged the King
to snuff out "those uppity scratchers."

What a school of art and verse, The House of Hathor

  Nor could any pluck the harp
  or beat upon a row of drums
  or pick with gentle squalls of notes
  'pon the nefer-guitar
  like the women & men there dwelling

What a school of music and drum, The House of Life of Hathor

  Beer was sacred to Hathor
  and every revel
  Save that of Apep.

  And ahhh the beer

  produced by the artists
  of Hathor

  sweet with dates
   the beer grew
    within the
   barley dough

  & the wine dripped lascivious
  out of the press
  best in the land.

Grumbles and whispers
swept the land con-
cerning the rites of Hathor
held in the House of Life.

All night long they drank
the sacred drool
All night long
the household danced for Hathor
who raised her skirt for angry Ra,
Hathor of the Horns.

The drummers incomparable and
twin-reed flutists urged the swirling,
the dancers shook the sistra
they shook the square tambourines
they clacked the ivory finger-cymbals

& Hathor of the Sycamores
walked toward Ra, and Ra sent
barques of servants underneath
to touch the stars of Hathor.
O rites of Hathor.

Meanwhile
Ammenemes I (1991–1962)
beginning of the 12th dynasty
transferred many artists down the
Nile from the area of Thebes to
Memphis, and notice was served upon

The House of Life of Hathor
to get ready to hit the bricks.

No one at the House of Hathor
wanted to leave sweet Thebes
for Memphis merely to cop
a scope on the "great Art of the past"
just because some jacked-off jackal
of a King desired to push their
minds, therefore their art, therefore
their muscles 4/5/600 years back
to 2600 B.C.

Ab-Mer was an artist lived
at Hathor's House of Life
Ab-Mer the painter/carver

And Ab-Mer was sorely angered
by the Pharaoh.
When he was
        alone
        he shouted
        the King's name

            He threw crocodile dung
            at the sun shouting
          "The worm eat the King!"

            Then, curse upon curse,
            Ab-Mer was fired from

his job as coffin-carver
at the royal snuff-works
for drawing
a weirdo version
of the King's cartouche
upon a fresh pine box,
drew an ear
where the sun-disk
should have been.
"Son of Ear!" his friends laughed
in the tented saloon,

"Here's a drink
to getting fired
for the carving
of the King's ear!!"

"A fist upon the king!"
"Hathor!" and all drank
and dancing the poets sang.

The sin of the writers, musicians
dancers, painters, stone workers &
"tasters of combinations" as some
were known who partook of several
skills—the sin in the authorities'
mind was that the House of Hathor
extended all such deific protection
from the kings and queens and
courtoids to all the people,

especially those at the Hathor
House of Life.

"We are the glyphs
    we are the people dancing
    we are the magic colors
        upon the green cedar planks
    we are the writers we are the
        curls of the melons of the gardens
    we are the people singing and
        singing on paper
    we *ARE* the ceremonies!"—
this was their attitude.
"The grain belongs to everybody"—
passed about on pot-pieces
for those who could read.

When Ab-Mer cursed the Pharaoh,
as common to any police state
the word drifted up the power-
climb adorned with grotesque
additions—The King was
afraid of the curse. What insolent
carver of coffins dared
trash the King? It will be noted
that the Pharaoh did wear a cobraic
uraeus on a hippie headband 'pon his
mantled brow which was designed
to handle and to ward off the
oncoming vibes of destruction.

Like kings of all time he never
quite trusted his defenses.
So he put out a contract for the
brick-out of Ab-Mer the caustic
carver, with a team of scowling
crude foreigners dwelling in a
tent town deep in marshes
south in Upper Egypt.

While the goons were floating
Down the Nile, Ab-Mer was singing
w/ men and women friends, passing
a paper roll by the cool lake
in the closed court-grove on
grounds of the House of Hathor,
upon which roll they all
were composing a satire-skit
about the King.

Moans of eager skin
leaked forth till a sword hooked
into the side of the tent
and the rude king's hit-men
started to chop, shouting
        "Where is Ab-Mer?"
"Ab-Mer we cut up your face?"—bodies
dashing in the garden
whence Ab-Mer somehow escaped, formulae
of hatred
boiling from his lips.

Late at night Ab-Mer
sneaked back into the compound,
to dance with I-mm-eti
the love of his life.

She wore a small stone Ab-Mer painted
with her portrait
as she shook.
He watched her dance, he danced also
and all the sistra-shakers, drummers
guitar-players surging for Hathor

I-mm-eti dipped back down
upon the dance platform
back bend, shimmy,
back bend

Ab-Mer loved the one who danced
there more than his heart
could bear
            almost.

And when their eyes met
eyes danced out of the sockets
and the eyes took off the eye-clothes
and one eye drew atop the other
and the eye-tongue slid upon the shiny eye.

Late late the chorus of Hathor sang
as I-mm-eti swayed and shimmied
bounced and leaped into exhaustion.

But after 15 minutes rest
the frazzle turned to frenzy
and torrid need
o'erwhelmed them.

I-mm-eti nodded him come to her rooms
where shards of his drawings ringed the walls
and poems they wrote made love upon the plaster.

And not since Isis taking the form of a bird
did hover above Osiris
to take him within
did such a love convulse upon the Nile
as I-mm-eti and Ab-Mer the outlaw
throughout the nighttime found Hathor
's wild flood
drowning the tramples of the spear-men
searching the marshes for Ab-Mer
cursed the Pharaoh.

But morning found the laughter of Hathor twisted to groan
and doomed with separation, danger, dread of death
Ab-mer slipped down the Nile, through the Delta, and off
to an island, crying every day for years and years
but losing the grasp of the love lost tragic

And I-mm-eti made a mistake
one night drunk on henek, the barley beer,
and the child grew within
and she was seized enslaved by a mean man
who smelled of burnt goose-feathers
for a life of never a dance.

Ab-Mer was able to return from exile 20 years later
during the senility of King Ammenemes I
but could not find his love

though he searched from cottage to tent to hut to house
both sides of the river
no one knew her, remembered or thought to find.

    And as for the Risen House of Hathor—
    when Ab-Mer returned it was many years
    since the great fire wiped that down into the
    sand   and the great art lay beneath the claws of
    the griffin vultures.

    And Ab-mer secured a position
    in another House of Life, more sedate
    more powerful, wealthy, modest
    where Ab-Mer became a staid bent disciple
    of rectitude. "I lost my chops"
    he'd moan beneath a load of
    wine, railing against the Nile-side water stick
    foreboding drought.

The aged drunken Ab-mer
lowered his weeping face to the table.

"Hathor!" he cried, "Hathor
I shall dance!" and
the old man
rose to dance, and dancing
tore some sinews
in his legs and
stumbled to the floor where
purple bruises spread
beneath his dry barked skin.

"I-mm-eti" whispered Ab-Mer
"O I-mm-eti."

HIEROGLYPHS

Each word a
flash-pod correspondent
to an event
in the Great Beyond
of the Yaru Fields
as in the
possibility of Coming Forth By Day

the hiero-symbol
↓   ↓   ↓   ↓   ↓

Keep that grain
swooning
Hathor, please!

THANATOIDAL
TRANSFORMATION
EQUATIONS

"Thou com'st out of thy grave every morning
  Thou return'st every evening

Thou passest through eternity in pleasure"

by the living swarmies
painted on papyrus

by the hiero-symbols
painted 'pon basalt

to the Beyond

 soul scroll

in a box
wrapped
in the mummy cloth
or stuck into the coffin

believing that
the words
and pictures

would insure transreal
grooviness for the snuffee

No greater belief in
words has there been.

BOOTY

Like a dog-breathed homunculus
the wizened child crawled along
the cedar sluice.

      squeaky rumbled the dyspeptic colon
      and no wonder so
      for they froze the growth
      kept the boy like a monkey
      fed vulture scraps

     "Gotta keep li'l Mek-mok small"
     quoth dad.

The cedar plank-tongue
slowly had slid 150 feet through Princess Her-Wetet's
mountain tunnel
not touching any sides or floor lest the trigger
tumble the mountain liths

His father, older brother, grandpa
waited at the sunlight
for the child to load the booty upon the sluice-sledge

Fruition! Fruition! the grandpa rubbed his hands in glee

     "We will
     pull out the plank
     the little brat
     will try to run
     out toward us, then . . ."

For 75 years the robber clan of Mek-Macrae
had tried to crawl

through Her-Wetet's smooth straight tunnel
into the Theban mountain

but the designer had fiendishly
set traps at regular spots
on the walls and ceiling and floor
that a light passing foot or pressure on the wall would
trigger an avalanche of adios,

tons of the mountain

        Mek-mok the boy had lost his uncle
        and uncle's uncle two different times
        they tried—dead in crush-liths.

The Tomb of Princess Her-Wetet,
Chantress of Amon:

Cedar sluice-tongue
'pon which the boy
crawled into
The Hall of Booty

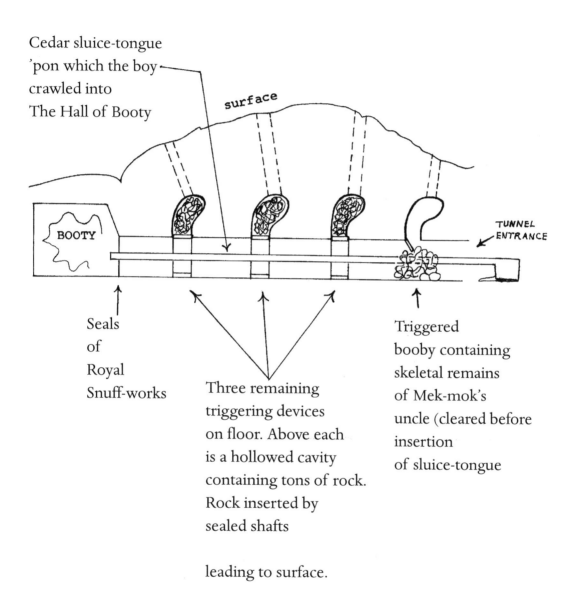

surface

BOOTY

TUNNEL
ENTRANCE

Seals
of
Royal
Snuff-works

Three remaining
triggering devices
on floor. Above each
is a hollowed cavity
containing tons of rock.
Rock inserted by
sealed shafts

leading to surface.

Triggered
booby containing
skeletal remains
of Mek-mok's
uncle (cleared before
insertion
of sluice-tongue

The finest Lebanese planks
built end to end
like a medical spatula
for some huge deity such as Ptah

with sides built
up with edging
(prevent the sledge
full of looting
    fall off the tongue
    trigger any rock-plop).

The boy crept through the murk with
tallow torches
       toward the moolah

along the well-oiled sluice
dragging the small sledge
150 feet of rope off either end.

    Mek-mok slowly loaded the satchels
    from the treasure room of Her-Wetet's tomb
    upon a sledge
    and the robbers at the entrance pulled
    it to the light
    then Mek-mok reeled the empty back for reload.

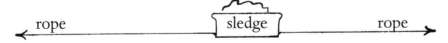

The boy was (slightly) daffy
mashed a miniature granary
with a ceremonial oar

     disturbed vibes
     upsetting the Princess
     by means of
     THANATOIDAL TRANSFORMATION EQUATIONS

     as she was plucking 'ternal wheat
     down on Paradise Farm

The Nubian reapers
bent in Yaru pleasure along side the Princess
     just as the boy was chopping up the tomb

fell down groaning
their mer-cutters splaying
     princess bent in agony

Robbers didn't care, they
sought the jewels, the gold
and yes   the precious oils

Mek-mok was sloppy
oil jugs rolled off the sluice
smashed
     one in particular indicating
     that the Princess was burned
     by the Regal Purveyor of scents—

not oil, but ooze unholy
village struck by flash-plague
such stench
phew!
eyes smarting, nose like snorting
ground-up brillo pad.

Mek-mok ice-picked the rubies from
the statues of the Princess

A scream of pain
in the grain fields of Heaven
"My eyes! my eyes!"   red pits
where eyes had.

Transformation   transformation.

"Canst 'ou see now
in the Yaru River bottoms
Princess dear? Hyuf hyuf hyuf" im-
portuned the griseous-fingered thief boy

pried the gold leaf off
the coffin sledge, broke the alabaster jars
dry friable guts of Her-Wetet
spilling on the row of sacred oars.

The rob-boy stuck a couple of gold wheat-stalks
into his mouth thinking of fangs,
laughed, "look at me! look at me!"

Will Her-Wetet walk a pauper through Elysium?
Forever adrift
                in a reed boat
reft of the total pleasure
promised by the words of the walls
down upon the howling banks of

the RIVER

REPORT

Council of Eye-Forms Data Squad

DATA!   DATA!

Subject: Her-Wetet
            Chantress of Amon

Case File: Dimension X°_{147}—44739J

Time: 1153 B.C.

Place: Necropolis, Thebes, Egypt

Subject was a Female Hamitic, 5′11″ Bl/Br approx. 140 lbs. age 37—cause of death: stampede of hippopotami. This writer attended various nodules of the embalming ceremonies. Subject was afforded a full 70 day spice-douse wherein subject's features were held remarkably intact.

A report of the Yaru Surveillance Team is attached below as *Appendix A*.

Imposition of the Netherworld Glyph (⊗) occurred in 70 days. During this period the coffins and artifacts were carved and painted. The texts of the Book of The Dead 'dorned with the fair beauté of Her-Wetet torrid chantress, were drawn up in 7 colors 'pon the wide papyrus scroll.

70 days to ⊗

Brain was hooked out through nose
   some of it dissolved via dissolve-gush poured within
     brain thrown away, no care fo' rotting data files

   heavy chop scene
    performed on bod

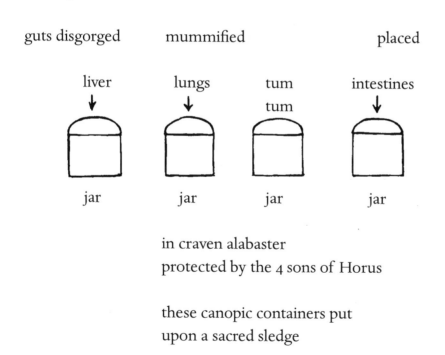

guts disgorged   mummified   placed

liver   lungs   tum   intestines
                 tum

jar   jar   jar   jar

    in craven alabaster
    protected by the 4 sons of Horus

    these canopic containers put
    upon a sacred sledge

post scrape-job re inner mush gush
cavity packed with pieces of natron salt
(sodium carbonate sodium bicarbonate
sodium chloride sodium sulphate)
wrapped in linen
                         suck up body ooze
                                   body drool
natron sprinkled on the outer also
—dry Egyptian climate helped the dry-out

After the jerkification, natron removed
body given water sponge bath
then rub-a-dubbed with resins coniferous
cavities packed with resin-soaked wads o' linen
—stuffed with taxidermist's care: "life! life!"

Stan Brakhage, Eye-Form Surveillance data-positor
filmed the sew-up
stone eye
             placed on chop-scar
             prior to the long winding

fingers, toes
wrapped separately
toe-stalls finger-stalls
of gold
             coatings of resins
             applied to coatings of linen
             175 yards of linen strips used
             to wrap the subject chantress
             Her-Wetet.

There was a slight
but savable error
—portion of the right ear
was discovered beneath
the chop bench
swept up, according to the
ceremony, with the spilt
desiccative and linen pieces extra,
buried in storage jars
near the mouth of her tunnel.

By barge procession
passed
right bank to left bank, Nile
down into the Valley of Salient Snuff

oxen pulled
the sledge

      mourners fisted dirt in poofs,
      self-beat, shrieks
      & long dinny moans

friends of Her-Wetet, plus
priests and servants
and porters with platters
of gifts.

By the edge of the tunnel
last ceremony
coffin
tipped on its end

"opening of the mouth"
that the chantress
yodel gently
down where the scoffers
cannot scoff

Priest in role as Deity
drove out the
devil dirt, like
            "out thou 𓏏𓊖𓏏-fiends
            out thou hitler verbs
            out moloch out nixon out
            of this voice!"

APPENDIX A.

Report: Yaru Surveillance Team
Subject: Princess Her-Wetet, Chantress of Amon

Eye-Form Surveillance Team
was required to utilize
Beckmanian
Transformation Nodes (via diagonal dimension dives)

in order   to hover behind
The Death Barque   while
still escaping the particularly wary wet-fanged
            attendant Deity known as Anubis

The jackaline Anubis
is thought to be able to undertake a nearly N-
dimensional scientia-sweep
so it was necessary to observe only from
dimensions he was unable to fathom.
Her-Wetet, The Chantress of Amon, was observed
in the rapids of showery rubicund petals just prior
to being sucked into the golden eyeball wherein the
petal torrent falls and disappears. It is stunningly
beautiful to see the soul-brain fall through the Eye.

Dimensional Adjustment Procedures enabled the
Eye-Form Surveillance Team to observe the Princess
arriving in the first sections of The Underworld.

When the rope of the Ferry was thrown ashore
a cat-headed goddess (holding a whip) led the singer
toward and through the so-called Door of Percipience.

Hallelujah
            the deceased   strolled quietly past
            42 fierce Spiritual Assessors

            Soul-jewel shining
                        no sin-grime cloying
                                        Hallelujah

            Osiris reached in between her breasts
            and brought out her heart

            Jackal-headed Anubis
            lifted her heart
                        upon the scales

                heart on one tray
                against the Maat feather
                on the other

                Little baboon jumping
                up and down on the mid pole

while Ibis-headed Thoth wrote down
the data on a tablet

Concomitant with the weighing
was the chanted enumeration of sins *NOT*
committed

(if th'accumulated sin-grime didn't tilt the
heart against the Feather then

Heaven!

but if it tilted, then soul, and it is confusing
here, would either a) be doomed to roam Earth

b) be consigned to the friends of
Adios Chew Devour
the so-called
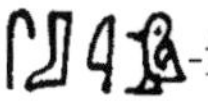-fiends
c) be eaten by a low slung
wrinkle-snouted Devourer
known as Am-Mut

d) all of the above.)

Blameless in truthful blessed bliss-out surged
the sinless Chantress of Amon when her heart
balanced the Maat

Osiris tucked it back within
her bounteous bosom

And the low slung
wrinkle-snouted slime gobbler Am-Mut
had to wait for ano'r time ano'r soul
to suck from the plate of truth.

Subject chantress then endured the marvel of The Final Purification
in the Lake of Fire
        guarded by 4 apes holding torches—

        4 torches extinguished
        in the 4 pails
        of Universal Milk . . .

        It is to be noted here
        that *ALL* this judgment was hard indeed to
        bring to surveillance:

        Shifting Forms . . .
        unable to
        jot them
        as they shift . . .

        Dream-Stream
        film just blurrs:

What is she doing?   The subject chantress and baboon
                         of Thoth adore The Solar Disk

No! No! Dummy!   The subject chantress is actually
                   bowing down before the supine
                   Deity: Crocodile Earth

Bull Shit!   The subject chantress is being led
                   by the triune Ptah-Osiris-Sokaris
                   for induction into the Mysteries

Hear the chant of the priests: "That she may
make all the transformations she desires"

Forms   Forms   Forms   Forms

Apparently jubilant over her new abilities
subject assumed a razzle-dazzle arpeggio
of weird forms:

                microbe, heron, swallow, ox,
                mollusk, rain storm, church
                steeple, projective verse

                what a dazzling sequence!

And more: subject Her-Wetet on Ra-raft
            subject Her-Wetet as Sky Bug
            then Ra-Hawk   Solar Disk
            Sun Flower   Cherry Blossom

She might have volunteered for a tour
of duty as an oarsperson
on the Solar Barque

but one of the strangenesses
of this particular paradise
is that they settle down, the souls,
to reap bright grain in a
brass-walled place
called The Yaru Fields

where the Spirits are precisely 10′6″ tall
where the grains are precisely 10′6″ tall
and the grain-ears precisely 3 feet long

said fields
located in the 2nd Arit (or Mansion)
of the 7 Arits
                    Underworld.

Accordingly, Her-Wetet settled down to a normal death
and walked toward Yaru.

There are twin sycamores
of malachite at the world's end
twixt which
                    Ra oozes forth

There is the Western Mountain
where Hathor Cow
goddess of necropolis

met the snuffee
saying "Hi!
the grain field's that way!"

Image shift: celestial bull and 7 kine
4 rudders of He'v'n
Shu muscling Nut off Geb

"Hi, Hathor!"—the soul of Her-Wetet
beaconed in thrillsome shifting tides
of form and form

Then Her-Wetet happ'ed to walk past
godly Osiris lying on his back
on the loamy mount of Khepri

The festal cone of Her-Wetet melts
in the fire of their pleasure
Her-Wetet atop the God
belly burning.

Subject chantress was not hesitant in fact frequently
to interrupt her wheat-cutting activities in the eons
thereafter and to run over to Khepri Mountain
and to effect unification with the Deity known as
Osiris (a Male Black, about 19′6″, weight approx. 430 lbs.,
with extremely bloodshot, maybe entirely rubicund, eyes;
wearing blue beard and blue wig; armed with flagellum)

Scarcely had subject
begun to work in the
sun wheat when subject
bent over   as if in pain
her eyes   looked like
the insides   of ketchup bottle caps

Subject winced—
The wheat field
where she and her
companions (unknown
Male Blacks wearing Nubian
wigs and armed with scythes)
were deep in harvest,
fell apart   in disarray.

        Dimensional Scan Operation
        indicated a forcible intrusion
        into her mountain tomb-tunnel
        by the robber clan known as
        the Mek-Macraes
        where certain stones were pried
        from votive statues, a
        model granary was beaten
        t'toothpicks therein.

Subject cantatrice rolled moaning down.
Her body bent
a long row of grain
with
        falling rolling
that the sun-wheat heavy
struck muffled gong sound
against the Yaru Walls of brass.

Subject stumbled forth
along the River Bank

"My Eyes! My Eyes!"

ISMAELI MUSLIMISM

65 years and 202 days since the Kaliyuga sunk in Lake Huron carrying a load of iron ore and a crew of sixteen. The seventeenth, John Murphy Second Mate had left the ship when it docked at Erie Pa. so that he could visit some friends in Buffalo. But the captain, impatient in his first year of command, left before he could get back and so under manning even more the already under manned ship. When the storm came, she couldn't get up enough steam to reach safety, in the giant waves.

The only part of the ship they found was the pilot house which had floated between the islands of Fitzwilliam and Cove, on eastwards into Georgian Bay.

		Adam
8th century	Muhammed ibn Ismail is the 7th Imam	
	to those who become Ismailis. God	
	will grant him Adam's paradise permitting	Noah
to	of things forbidden and all things created	
	in this world.	
		Abraham
10th	7 is big. Seven heavens and holes in head.	
is SACRED	Time as cycles. An Annunciator starts each	Moses
HISTORY,	period, followed by an Executor and seven	
	Imams.	
		Jesus
	Live at the end of Muhammad-as-annunciator-	
	era. Waiting for 7th and new era to happen.	
		Muhammed
HIERARCHIES	Ecclesiastical: Annunciator, Executor Imams,	
	12 Hojjats for the 12 regions of the world, da'is,	
	and initiates.	

Spiritual: 1) God
            2) The Word Kun "Be"
            3) Angels

1) GOOD FORTUNE	2) OPENING	3) VISION
Directs to pleasure	Resolve	Project so they
of God thru proper	ambiguous	continue after you
knowledge.	verses and	leave earth. A
	put in	must for ultimate
	proper place.	happiness.

GNOSIS,   A man who can acquire gnosis can be saved. Sacred
               knowledge is the inner not public possession of the outer
               scriptures. To know only the apparent is death. To know the
               inner is life.

               Science of letters.

Gorgani's CHAIR	FIELD	TOMB
Exoteric religion.	Initiation to philosophy is RESURRECTION.	Death of exoteric and life of philosophy.

10th Sijistani adds the logic of Neo-Platonism
to what comes before. E.g.,

God
        Intellect
                Soul
                        Nature
                                Fathers of Spheres
                                        Mothers
                                                Their mating gives
to   mineral
                                                        vegetable
                                                        animal
                                                        rational

12th 11th century ends with separation between
the Yemeni and Alamut Ismailis.

The Yemenis took a lot of their stuff from
Kirmani who wrote in the 10th-11th century.

Tawheed	Tanzeeh
Unique double negatives. E.g., God is not such and such and He is not not such and such.	Specific spiritual and terrestrial limits, as manifestations of the Absolute.

Theophanism

Call of #1 Intelligence to
all forms of light is the eternal convocation. Ismailism
is the terrestrial form of it. On earth we begin with the
initial Adam who is before the Adam of our cycle.

#2 Intelligence
complied with #1 as first emanation.

#3 Intelligence
proceeded from the first two. He reacted by refusal and opposition. This
was the Spiritual Adam, bewildered. He refused the limit which preceded
him, #2, because he didn't see that if this limit limited his field of vision, it
also referred beyond. He believed it was possible to attain the inaccessible
principle without this intermediary limit because he misconceived the mys-
tery of the God revealed in #1. He thought that this would identify #1 with
the absolute deity. To flee this "idolatry" he got caught up in the absolute
and succumbed to the worst metaphysical idolatry. When he finally got free
of this stupor, he rejected far from him the demonic shadow of Satan in the
inferior world where he reappeared from cycle to cycle of occultation. But
then he saw himself delayed, fallen behind himself. From #3 Intelligence he
became #10. This interval measured the time of his stupor. It corresponded
to the emanation of 7 other Intelligences called the 7 Cherubim or 7 Divine
Verbs who helped the Spiritual Adam recome to himself. The 7 indicated
the ideal distance of his downfall. The time was his delay on himself. It was
the retarded eternity.

Each of the Cherubim had a pleroma of forms of light. All these com-
posed the pleroma of Spiritual Adam. They were immobile with him in the
same delay. In his turn he extended to them the convocation. Most refused

his offer. This darkened the essential depth of the beings of light. Spiritual Adam understood that if they lived in the spirit world, they would never be delivered from their shadows. Therefore he himself became the demiurge of the physical cosmos as the instrument by which each of the forms would find its salvation.

Because they were terrified of their own shadows, they started a triple movement in order to extract themselves. This resulted in the three dimensions of cosmic space. The most dense mass was stabilized at the center. Cosmic space burst forth in several regions: the celestial spheres and the elements. Each planet in its turn governed a world during a millennium until the seventh, the cycle of the moon. Then the first terrestrial man appeared on earth surrounded by his companions. This Adam and his 27 companions were located at Ceylon. He was the epiphany and veil of Spiritual Adam. His cycle was an era of happiness where the human condition even in its physical part was that of paradisiacal beauty. He perceived spiritual realities directly and not under the veil of symbols. He was the founder of a permanent esoteric hierarchy which was uninterrupted in cycle after cycle until Islam and after. Resurrection on resurrection until the restoration of #3.

1164

(August 8)

GRAND RESURRECTION for the Alamut Ismailis. The Imam Hasan said of the divine Imam: "Our Lord is the resurrector; He is the Lord of all beings; He is the Lord who is the act of the absolute being; He excludes all existential determinations because He transcends all; He opens the threshold of His mercy and by the light of His knowledge makes all beings be seeing, hearing and speaking for all eternity."

He who knows himself knows his Imam.

The Imam has said: "I am with my friends wherever they seek me, on the mountain, in the plain and in the desert. Those to whom I have revealed my essence, that is to say the mystical knowledge of myself, do not need a physical proximity. And this is the GRAND RESURRECTION."

Now   Suhrawardee who cannot be connected exoterically   1180s
             with the Ismailis resurrects.

THE STORY OF WESTERN EXILE

The Shaykh, Imam, knower, gnostic, unique of his age, shaykh of his time, Shaykh Shihab ad-deen Suhrawardi, Allah holy his soul and lumen his grave, said:

Praise Allah, the Lord of both worlds. Peace for his servants whom he chose, especially for our chief Muhammad, the chosen, as well as for his people and his companions.

Now then, when I saw the story of Hayy ibn Yaqzan, I noticed that the wonders of its deep symbols lacked any reference to the great state which is the greatest even contained in the divine books, in the symbols of the philosophers or hidden in the story of Salaamaan and Absaal which was written by the writer of Hayy ibn Yaqzan. It is the secret from which emerge the plateaus of the people of tasawwuf and the possessors of revelation. But it was only referred to in the recital Hayy ibn Yaqzan at the end where it was said: "Sometimes individual men emigrate to him." I want to talk about it by way of a story I have named The Story of Western Exile for some of my respected brothers. I confide in Allah my intention.

When I was traveling with my brother Aasim, the guardian, from Transoxiana to the Western Land, we were hunting a flock of birds on the coast of the Green Sea. We were taken by surprise in the "country whose inhabitants are oppressors," i.e., Qairawaan. When its people saw us approach unwary and that we were sons of the Shaykh known as the Guide son of the Excellent Yemenite, they grabbed and bound us in chains and irons and imprisoned us in a bottomless pit. Over this dead end pit which they filled with our presence was a high castle with many towers. They said, "It won't be held against you if you climb up the castle as two pure ones when you want to. But near morning there is no escape from the pit."

It was really dark, there in the pit. When we held out our hands we could scarcely see them. But in the evening we climbed up the castle and were two high ones looking out of a small window on the sky. Sometimes doves came to us from the forest of Yemen, giving news of the sanctuary. Occasionally a bolt of Yemenite lightning flashed on us from the right eastern side, informing us of what was happening in Nejd. The winds of Iraq overflowed so much ecstasy on us that we longed for our homeland.

So, at night we were above and by day below until we saw a Hoopoe come in the window, greeting us one moonlight night. In his beak a note saying: "From a bush in a holy place on the right side of the valley." He said to us, "I know how you'll be freed. I brought you an 'announcement of certainty from Sheba' and it is expressed in a note from your father."

When we read the note, it said that it was from the guide your father and: In the name of Allah the compassionate, the soother. We made you desirous, you didn't feel the longing. We called you, you didn't leave the West. We gave you a sign, you didn't understand. If you and your brother want to be freed, don't be slow to start your journey. Keep your hands on our line. The sphere of the holy celestial body predominates over the borders of the eclipse. When you reach the "valley of the ants," shake your skirt and say, "Praise Allah who made me live after making me die 'and to Him the resurrection' and destroy your family." Kill your wife, "She was supposed to stay behind." Pass where you are commanded because "Those will be completely cut off in the morning." Get on the boat and say, "It will set sail and will anchor in the name of Allah."

He depicted in the note everything which would be on the way. Then the Hoopoe went ahead. The sun nooned over our heads. We reached the edge of the shadow. We got in the boat. It sailed "in waves like mountains." We wanted to ascend Mt. Sinai to see the secluded place of our father.

There rolled between my son and I "the wave and he was drowned."

I knew that "the deadline for my people was in the morning. Is not the morning near?" I knew "the town where they were committing evils would be turned upside down" and it would rain "on them heavy rocks, downpour."

When we came to a place where the waves were crashing and the water rolling, I took my wet nurse who had suckled me and threw her in the open sea.

We were traveling in a boat "having planks and caulking." But we tore it apart, fearing a king beyond us who was angrily grabbing every boat.

The loaded boat passed by us by the islands of Gog and Magog to the left side of Mt. Ararat. There were some fairies in front of me and a fountain of molten brass under my control. I said to the fairies, "Blow on it so that it becomes red hot." Then I created a barrier from it to separate myself from Gog and Magog.

"The premise of my Lord is true" proved true.

I saw the bald summits of Aad and Thamood on the road. I walked in that region. "It was completely desolate."

I took the two heavy weights with the heavenly bodies and put them along with the fairies in a long necked bottle which I made round. On it were lines like circles.

I shut off the streams from heaven's liver. When the water was shut off from the mill, the building collapsed. The air escaped to the air. I threw the celestial body of celestial bodies upon the heavens so that it crushed the sun, the moon and the stars.

I escaped from the fourteen powers and the ten tombs from which the shadow of Allah was created in order to pull me to his holy sphere easily after he created "the sun for their guide."

I saw the path of Allah and understood that this is the straight one.

I carefully covered my sister and my family "with the robe of Allah's torment" so that she spent the night in its dark part. She was frenzied by it. The nightmare reached an awful pitch.

I saw a lamp which had oil in it. A light was shining from it which was cast around the house. Its niche was blazing. The inhabitants of the house were lit up from the shining of the sun's light on them. I put the lamp in the mouth of a dragon living in a tower of a labyrinth under which is the Red Sea and above which are the stars whose rays no one knows except their creator and "those who are well-grounded in knowledge."

I saw the Lion and the Bull who had been invisible up until then and the Crab who had been in the fold of the rotation of the celestial bodies and the Balancer behind the slender woven clouds which the spiders of the elemental world webbed in the world of becoming and corruption.

There was a ram with us. We left him in the desert. The earthquake destroyed him and the lightning's fire struck him.

When distance was cut and the road ceased to be "and water welled out of the conic shaped oven," I saw the high bodies. I went up close and heard their tones and melody. I learned their reciting poetry. The sounds rang my ears like the sound of a chain being dragged on a solid rock. My nerves were almost severed and my joints separated from the pleasure it gave. This event continued to bear on me until the clouds were scattered and the placenta torn.

I exited from the caves and grottos so that I left the containing chambers, turning to the fountain of life. I saw a big rock sitting like a big mountain on the peak of the mountain. I asked the fish gathered in the beneficial pleasing fountain in the shadow of the great height: What is this mountain? What is this rock?

One of the fish who had taken up their way in the sea as a group answered. He said, "That is what you wanted. This mountain is Mt. Sinai. The rock is the secluded place of your father." I said, "And who are those fish?" He said, "Your image. You are sons of one father. They have a situation like yours and are therefore your brothers."

When I heard this and checked it out, I embraced them. I rejoiced over them and they rejoiced over me. I ascended the mountain and saw our father, a great shaykh who was on the edge of heaven and earth which were being split by the appearance of his light. I was amazed by him. I walked up and he greeted me. I bowed. I was on the verge of perishing in his shining light.

I cried for a while and complained to him about the confinement of Qairawaan. He said to me: "Take it easy. You are safe. But you have to go back to the western prison and the shackles you had removed so well." When I heard his words, my *aql* flew out and I moaned, crying the scream of someone about to die. I pleaded with him. He said, "Even though you have to go back, there are two reasons for you to be happy: When you go back to the prison it will be possible for you to return to us with ease whenever you want. Second, you will be saved in the end, abandoning the western land with its prison completely."

I rejoiced over what he said. Then he continued, "Know that this is Mt. Sinai. Above it is the dwelling of my father and your grandfathers. I don't relate to him unless you relate to me. We have other ancestors until the line ends up with my king who is the greatest grandfather, who has no grandfather and no father. All of us are his servants. By him we are illuminated and from him we acquire knowledge. He has the greatest beauty, the highest majesty, and the most overwhelming light. He is the high of the high, the light of lights, and is beyond light forever. He is the manifestor of every thing, 'And every thing perished except his face.'"

I was involved in this story until my state changed. I fell down from the sky into the pit among people who are not believers, imprisoned in the country of the west. Some pleasure stayed with me, but I can't describe it. I cried and prayed and was distressed because of my separation. That comfort was short-lived, passing quickly.

Allah delivered us from the chains and shackles of nature. "Say, praise Allah who will show you his signs and you will recognize them. Your Lord is watching over all your actions." "And say, praise Allah. But most of them are ignorant men." Peace for his prophet and his family.

End of the story of western exile.

THE MOON

balls out, stuck in the dark billow. The tree limbs are black shadows. Star specks 1 2 3 4, count. Sleep torpors heavy, the limbs weighted.

Eye awake. Ear confined to the walls inside. Outside fill to the sound of space. Each step an event. Shorewood drawn in along the river. The hill holds back shore woods below the raw plains floor.

Up there bare base where no thing stands equal to the sky expanse.

The moon and stars predominate. The earth has little enough to meet the heavens without the stripping, the flat black mud.

2

Mooney cut his hold. Sold his land for one million. Chased his sister hanging the shotgun over the rise. His farm stands alone overwhelmed by power lines. The hurst smooth prefabs of the landless predominate. They will have it all soon.

3

Tonight I call up the old earth anew. Glaciers recede, leave fingers of moraine new on the old bed rock contour. Limestone is wise in the he river bank cleft. I release the marine life cemented in lime.

The ancient sea laps back. Tropical fertility restores.

April 5, 1971 midnight

this thumb
skin scraped
off the knee of it.
Hard to heal place
for the wet to
set—crystallize to scab.
The scab pinched and
ooze out more as glue
to patch the scab.
Add one more layer
crusted and dried
to soften and wash away
in the bath.

                    October 2, 1971

    Nizaamee raising the dust of Iran. No other place. Why Sikander ? He
the only one he sees in the mirror.
    Wisdom of Alexander the Great. The unification of the ancient world.
Nizaamee doing it for mother earth as old Zoroaster.

                    June 3, 1971   10:15 A.M.

4 times Erie howled.
4 times they puked that night
in the fishing barge off Sturgeon Point.

Oh toilet
I'll never forget
yr calm lucid eye
and sweaty cool girth
for hugging.

6/20/71

In the beginning was BILLION born of THOUSANDS the rich daughter of
old HUNDRED great white father cloud ONE

round headed babe gangling
encased in PLACENTA smooth lined womb the umbilical river meander-
ing flows thru the slick melting thighs of GLACIER icy bridge a heave & a
snort.

Her son's wedding invitation reads:

GRAVEL SANDWORKS
&
LIMESTONE CRUSTACEA

their calcite son
CONCRETE.

June 20, 1971

He sat in the living room.
He the aql
SAT the soul
in the LIVING ROOM
separated from HE
the director.
SAT trying to get back
to HE
in the LIVING ROOM.
The only way back
is reentering the small SAT gate
gap between here and there,
the farther away.
What would it take
to be there = a city
all at once ?
Thus he sat in the room in the city ?
No, only opens a wider gap
than walls of a room.
The borders of a city e.g. L.A.
farther than you can see
and I needn't go into nation.

October 17, 1971

Wide awaking the white blend the smear crimson then baby gold through spaces of dark green lattice bastioned by dark dead trunk is where the hikmat alishraq ends.

Oct 4 dawn 1971

Only Tahmuras
you find riding
so hotly the
deev of writing
all over the world.

Riding something
as big as glacier
digging ridges
and piling up
moraine fingers.

October 29, 1971

Yes this flux but the tumblers do fall into place.

The sun cleanses the night but is worn out by noon and thrown away leak-
ing slightly as the half life divides itself over the infinitesimal in twilight.

Then no matter how hard you try and find a trace there.

Set the tumblers to lock on night constellations.

October 29, 1971

DIWAN

The inner gate
leads to the court.
The stream up the middle
leads to the pool.

Black now
the silver tarnished
out west.

Give it the glow
of the golden wall.
Gold backdrop
lights up all in front.

Summer St. is honest, ends at the cottage
like Sunset Bay one and the Dupage used to
soothe the sand in the days these were
summer resorts.

October 28, 1971

Heavy downpour.
Lightning blast through the trees
glowing as the gold backing of the
Persian miniature and the silver
of the Florida postcard.

Silver for Florida cypress garden.
Gold for Iranian garden cypress.

    8/24/71

   It is only clear the paratac must be kept to as Firdowsee had to work for
people to listen and Nizaamee to the silent majority of glaciers in a past
disconnected from connection in relivability with the present.

    8/24/71

The trucks hummed on 55
with the fervor of the giant dragonflies
in the tropical forest.
Not "any" tropical forest
but the one set place.
You know how trucks sound
around your house.
But the ones here
raise the dragonflies
of the rainforest
on the swamps of Lake Chicago.

The weed that looks like clover with longer stem red and lighter clove I pulled from the backyard below the stone level on August 24, 1971 at 3:00 P.M. There being behind what had been weeded before and ahead what was overgrown with weeds whom I sympathize with this clover like dairy plant who looks creamy clover with yellow butter flowers.

You stood there for two months maybe before that on bare ground never plowed deliberately left to the oaks of Searles who held it below his farm 30 ft. to the de-elevation so remarkable in a sea of single bean-like soy beans but with unbeanlike round leaves.

The corn emerges at intervals where it was impossible at the time of soybean planting to get it out. Corn grass stalks up which even with its greater chloroform has turned brown in the drought so leaving it in the condition of the oak trees whose inner core is a dead but solid wood support for the green leaving stem which only sometimes will be cut and grow new roots in wet sand with the proper moisture and shade.

8/24/71

The tendril of the gourd vine
grabbed hold of the near dead
marigold to pull itself along
the ground. Further growth
and flowers being the main
principle of advancement.
There was only one marigold
to attach itself to
in the direction of its growth.
And certainly the pumpkin plant
did not discriminate

over which gourd it would encircle
with its own growing tendril
as Black Hawk was made to realize
when squeezed by the tendril
of advancing pioneer farming
whose principle of squaring off
the available land for ownership
followed the course of the
Illinois and Michigan Canal
when it opened a vehicle
for flow into the land
once living under fear of Black Hawk.
It was situational
the way he was used
who crossed the Mississippi
for very different reasons
than were used to wage
a war of tendril land ownership.
Its corn and soybeans
now browning in the drought
to be investment fodder
on the open market
we have as fruit
of said growth principle.

8/24/71

Garshasp places at the edge of Hilmand river below the falls a thousand men high.

Over flows Ardvi Sura water goddess and so wisdom.

Falls of sperm to the sea foam. Ardvi Sura Maid of the Mist.

She the Iris flower lucid with the dew. Garshasp the burst forth on Sindab Ceylon and the Western Isle.

Iranian sperm covered the known seven climes.

Bibliography

Walker, Paul; Notes I took down from him on Friday morning Dec. 10, 1971, on Sijistani and early Ismailis.*

Ipsiroglu, M.S. *Painting and Culture of the Mongols*. Harry N. Abrams, Inc., New York. See page 65 for full color reproduction of "Presentation of a Town."

Corbin, Henry. *Histoire De La Philosophie Islamique*. © 1964, Paris, pp. 110–152.

_____. *Opera metaphysica et mystica*, II. Teheran and Paris, 1952. pp. ∠VO–∠9V.

And whatever is in your library by W. Ivanow and Henry Corbin.

* What does retard is the second of the categories of the translation which Paul mentioned to me. That was the Mushin Mahdi method of Harvard University where there is one English word for every Arabic or Persian. Which makes perfect "translations" for the "community of academics" all over the world. And I don't think it is more but less accurate. Every one of the important works has been read by somebody who could translate but didn't because of the smell in the hoses of Turkish water pipes.

ALCHEMY

It was for this reason, to understand the nature of possibility, that I long ago left my laboratory for the tables of fortune looking for new numbers of older times still waiting to win knowing that what we are dealing with is a synchronism of the past 1,000,000 years preparation—so we are the lords of fortune for a different time and unless we deal properly in the giving and taking of elements now, a future consciousness will be stuck in a syndrome that doesn't even concern them—someone else's unfinished business—as in the case of the value of archaeology to the dreams of children—otherwise those cities would not live. But the new sensibility applied to the wreck of what went before will only need the vaguest memory to produce an element of earthly evidence of it all which was perhaps needed or known but, in fact, never present, owing to the syncopations of creation and evolution. Why, otherwise, should we turn our homes into museums or space stations? Are the dice not in the same corner as the snake?

I see the Alchemist as the proper director of the actions of meeting places, acting on the spot with the knowledge of the threads that bind all energies in hand. The overseer of the gift of many winds come down to the fire, each giving and taking according to its powers, fashioning a jewel, hence to be of forgotten origin, marking the meeting of a certain time and space whose elements would never otherwise survive. So, we have the natures of various metals and stones to act as a backlog to fields of mind, the particular nature of earth to allow us to return to the way of their making—their use is no other. The elemental power of echo the weight of the mountain holds to the exclusion of all other men.

It is the Alchemist's task also to realize the directness of the situation at hand (or the one he contemplates creating) and the elements it deals with excluding what they have been mixed-up with before, since the whole dance cannot be taken into account if we are to get that foot that kicked what we want not to somewhere else, because none of it is lost, really.

Our existence, being more than random, will necessarily project order as essence within the attributes of its own nature so that process remains a pre-eternal fact and complexity generative to the extent of velocity. Hence the creation of the base, or formulated from the subtle, or nominal—a gas—via a series of screens providing a map (a scene of the possible), energy routes by which refinement with the preservation (Keys to the Kingdom) or renewal (The Fountain) of certain energy forms is possible. This is what I call the heroics of proportion—the insistence of certain patterns to trans-mit in a certain way or to recreate themselves at a new level, while still hold-ing to their base forms as original necessity (not having recourse to another order)—a constant process of reduction and adornment.

"How—maybe in the lakes we have mentioned—out of a collection of all sorts of organic molecules there originated systems, i.e., living organ-isms that for once possessed contrivances for a) reproduction and muta-tion and b) provision of energy for more complexity demanding negative entropy, we do not know. We can quite speculatively think of the regulating cooperation of crystals having large elementary cells and high absorption power, like, for example, zeoliths." Unsold, The New Cosmos.

A scientist's view of the Philosopher's Stone, that creation having the wisdom of finding the pattern or earth intelligence—energy factor and assimilating all the elements without taking them from their field so that a process or inversion, or reversion, the Alchemist's key to transformation, should always be possible. It is a principle of clarity—fire to air—or water making that difference of light whereby it created life in salt by making it (the light) fluid, electric, viable and where it did not but retained the pos-sibility of anything—any arrangement—'in stasis'.

As in the evidence of language where certain elements are preserved in the nomenclature of mentality (not words) as next to each other or con-nected, though not perceivably because of their extension. Once these things are apprehended, logical determination will fight the originating nexus or causal centrum, taking space differently than before—it is what might be called the demonstrative imperfect which, like the clumsiness caused by gravity, the Alchemist always seeks to rectify. Also, in this respect, is the trouble caused (especially nowadays) by symbolic interference, where the proximity of a governing factor is taken to hold force over that which is close to it whether or not this is the field of its function—the truth of the matter being that elements are conjoined by the patterning gathered of large distances rather than the understandings caused by the relativity of current use, a kind of energy which the Alchemist must get underway before it becomes obstructive, or destructive in the sense that it cannot deal with the spirit it contains. Therefore,

the Alchemist must proceed with distillation of sublimation to release a primary nature from the complexities and weight its energy has incurred. Here it becomes obvious that transmutation is the necessary dream of escaping total confusion—finding the element that retains its power, attracting anything and being stuck with nothing. That knows the whole world and is shaped like a ring.

THE PLATES

I

The glass at first, the silica vessel—water glass to grow a garden of metal. The first matter, assemblage from the flood, a broken wheel in motion. Whirlpools in the tao, washes of experience.

II

The car of mercury, enabling us, for the moment to leave the sole of the road—whatever speed or combination gets back to you with your wing.

III

Providing present energy to conform to its counterpart by providing a third, all-pervasive element so that an equal reduction is possible and also so that options to conformative action may be excluded. So, night and day are of a common realm whose child is to understand each as three.

IV

That in terms of other things light is a solid, like gas, without weight, and has variances to itself.

V

The marriage of elements—channeling of radiances. The wisdom of the mountain being present in the garden.

VI

The tomb of glass or incubation allowing for the growth of self-nature with light as the only means of transference. It is also suggestive of the perfection of death. The crystal ship of guiding the unknowing, sleeping, of unhearing.

VII

Reduction of unnecessary elements by heat energy.

VIII

Forms of light in their proper proportion as in a rainbow, of the Dew of Heaven.

IX

The black crow, messenger of the unreturned presiding at the process of crystallization. Darkness as the guardian of mystery.

X

Revelation of the crystal to the world, its reception of airs of essences to initiate its use. The holding of power over moon as crow, the messenger, and snake, the motion or volition-encompassing. In the background is the tree of many worlds, hanging moons of all reflections as differentiated from what is known as the tree of jewels, usually a sign of death. The white stone, delivering from a single source multiple proportions, its curative power in the mixture of waters in which it was born. The Lion holds it between his paws, it makes the horse work.

XI

Transmitting through the crystal—the sowing of element to world-mind, understanding the transformations of nature. This being done in the presence of the master who can say what will grow to the dimensions of your use.

XII

Separation of the elements thus transmitted or their capture. Hermes shoots the new sun god before he can burn the world.

XIII

Rearrangement of new elements having passed through all human activity reduced to certain other elements wherein the gods can be seen as singing their anthems, invoking their ways.

XIV

This brings (the anthem) proper new arrangement of the other elements.

XV

Providing a suitable base or body to contain the new harmony.

XVI

Rendering confrontation of the produced attitudes to their proper subjects.

XVII

Mix those harmonies with those parts of the most holy to which they accord. The return to heaven by reverence and putting away as gathering spirit.

XVIII

Reunite those factors without disrupting those natures which they have attained in the process of age (reverence as distinct from separation). It is the feat of containing the jewel or a creative force in the lion's mouth or belly.

XIX

Sublimate the whole.

XX

Crowning the child of the creation, maintaining his heaven and the objects of his instruction.

XXI

The Emerging Queen.

NOTES TO THE PLATES

[transcribed from conversation March 1972, Buffalo New York]

The Alchemists are guardians of The Mountain and of The Garden—the process happening in The Garden—ultimately so that knowledge induced by The Snake, or say The Snake Himself, won't go hairy—so that the conditions of proportion won't be upset. The elements at hand, to find the place where they properly meet. The plates just show what kind of ground there is—picture-events—as far as The Kingdom of Alchemy is concerned. It could be anything, but the important part is that you have an actuality—which is the dream and not something made up, as figures arranged as a purposeful symbol. So that the actual alchemical processes are to reenact, in fact, the nature of the dreams. The idea is to capture the same nature—the jewels of his travel.

---

1   The Alchemist presents or coalesces the jewels (being the elements) of his travel. His language is 'metallic' only in the sense of activity—space and substance as productive of each other. Hence the relations of the basic metals to the planets and celestial 'spheres', meaning realms, each guarded by one of the great beasts—the bird, dragon, horse, lion, and gorgon (often one of these is replaced as a woman). To keep these beasts is the Alchemist's Work, as well as guarding the creations of their dance, since few understand the relationships between them.

2   A certain set of elements that stimulates you as to what you have to do that day, that would be your mercury.

3   You do what is necessary in the first place—never opt out for anything better.

4   Light has become almost a commodity!

5   The Alchemists come and go as the proper messengers of the precious and mundane and their relationship.

6   As your house, or as your mind as long as you keep these things in your mind.

7   Heat is to create light or fluidity, also truth.

8   Feed-back, as musicians have found, is useful, is effective because affective—it returns in clearer form, so it's like giving something away.

9   What comes to reap the harvest after the storm, being the volatile substance.

10   The stable radiating factor—on Earth, a concrescence, universally spread-out.

11   The accomplishment of sleep—the one, most important, missing element, the x factor that can do anything (any small source of energy).

12   Assailing the sun-angel properly, so that he will be bound on Earth again.

13   A further mission to perform!

14 I had that feeling when I wake up in the morning, if I stay in bed too long the birds start laughing at me.

15 A deduction from the vanity of time—so that there shall be neither waste nor excess of elements.

16 The realization that destruction yields creation.

17 Where things belong.

18 Understanding by common emotion—the lion is capable of devouring the universe with understanding.

19 Lotus-born, born from the Blue Lake—the power of bringing elements that aren't present into presence (like from 'the past', something new—to someone else—you make of it what you will).

20 The Great One will appear once you have manifested his activity on Earth—like preparing a feast.

21 Perhaps a young girl, because she isn't so old as to pass over things with the assurance of sophistication but rather dealing with them directly.

THE ALCHEMIST OF HUMANITY

The nature of the universe is that a transmutation is happening so constantly that the words element are a condition of perception rather than state of being—synchronizing the flow of mind and the external flow of activity as it sharpens itself to mind, or as mind is open to it—so that the concern is more with import rather than anything such as atomic structure (difference of experience) be what dissolves the elements of your existence the next day—but what to get is the wind, the gold is everywhere.

The function of the Alchemist of Humanity is to dictate, what kind of elements are to be brought into play. He shows what happens within any range of possibilities, what could have occurred, and to take the things that will work. The Holding Power: the actual purpose of the elements in your life as to your use of them to the exclusion of excess amounts to ultra-violet in the Kingdom so that life may live. It's your duty, on Earth, to find the other elements that go with it. You won't perceive elements unless they are constituent with your being or unless their force is such that they make an impression on your being. You still have an image, something that all the elements of your existence strive to create, new spirits and new elements to constantly feed or stabilize their changing condition. It's as if you were making up for a Noh drama.

PERSPECTIVE

ut oculus ad colores-
auris ad sonos,
ita mens homonis
non ad quaevis sed ad
quanta intelligenda
condita est.

—KEPLER

as eye to color
ear to sound,
so the mind of man is
conducted, not
to what it seeks but to
intelligible measures.

A contemporary biographer of Brunellesco tells us how he made a painting of the *Piazza* of San Giovanni, diminishing all the lines in accordance with his mathematical rules; and then, in order to establish the position of the spectator, he made a hole in his picture at the vanishing point. The spectator looked through this hole from the back and saw the picture reflected in a mirror which was placed at the exact distance of Brunellesco's original point of view. Thus perspective achieved *certezze*. But there was one element in landscape which could not be brought under control: the sky. The continual flux of change in the sky can only be suggested from memory, not determined by mathematics; and Brunellesco, perfectly realizing the limitations of his own approach, did not attempt to paint the sky behind his Piazza, but put instead a piece of polished silver.

—Kenneth Clark

Michael the handsomest
kid in the neighborhood
throwing our labelless
can denting it
useless : "IT'S CON
SIDERED EMPTY"

on, you huskies

    when he got through smiling
    nothing was left to say.

    he broke the sonic barrier
    in a jet-propulsion plane.

    it was a Buick.
    no one knew what to expect.

    go ahead I'll be your Spectre
    Jack said standing behind me.

    the first thing to be overcome,
    the memory of the Golden Age.

even lost in the woods one circles,
looking to backtrack or outguess

a tangle lies before us.
nobody needs to get lost.

in gardens hedges keep us apart,
shivers of forest woo us.

huddle in galleries, muse,
follow noses, walk the walls away.

fold the moment rightly, stick it in.
moving aside a star to see heaven.

panorama
11.28.73

·

a chrysanthemum

balanct upon its cut stem

the famous swordsman

PETRARCH'S MOUNTAINEERING EXPEDITION

there's nothing sentimental
about altitude.

the ears clear out,
avalanches lush down
over a whisper.

white-out they call it,
snowblind in a heavy blow.
"because it's there".

there's tiny spiders
in the upper atmosphere.

———————————————————

it's said to lightning out.

the glance of a man
in the ruined towns
conducts himself
always the same.

his marathon

into the oblong dark,
the first person.

breathing rarest air

HOME

in the final stages, your shadow
falls off & covers the earth.
you call it night. the heart
slows, white
cypress of the body.

married to the sky,
a glimpse of branches,
clouds,
driving him crazy.
into a gang of stars.

these are the flight
of far birds
over the water.
glowing as seen in war.
cold, as seen in crowds.

& the night
none go forth in,
alone,
fire a dark heat.
deep in the underground.

SOFT SHOULDERS

in all the stories they make love in
it's impenetrable night or daisies pied

just the same the sense of violation's
most enjoyable particularly alibied

however faithful two true lovers are
each other's eyes are all their eyes look for

and against that gentle light as against unbid surprise
each lover lives that neither lover dies

OUTLINES

in a safe act
such as woman
secure
in perspective
& a stranger's cares

estates in profile
yielding again
their human eyes

the full delineation
singly
unmistakable to face
invisible
from place to place

she gestures
absently enough,
the entire room

20° OUT SONNET

your perfect ears, your smiles, send to Cathay
in vain for their originals: further
than the stars, lightheaded men might say;
daringly, I say light as a blown feather.

all a slope of flowers those perfections are,
to balance through & tumble along in,
light-hearted, wind braiding your strong hair
and loosening a dress of blue satin.

no flower shivers in the fear of rain
or blue sky trembles at a wisp of cloud;
each smile newly smiled smiles again;
the sun washes blush and blouse out.

anywhere we might have gone we might still go;
anyone we might have known we might still know.

SEASCAPE WITH CLOUDS

down the sea for sailing men
the only woman aboard of wood
laid breast to wave and sounded

more to mark the disappearances
bodies gradual as days advance
a dim seascape with clouds recorded

coarse devotion salts the gentle mouth
fingers care what time they take in soft
lieu of a lover till love is an empty crown
adventurers order and outfit all their lives for

the night falls easily from star to star
the navigator envies his position
the sea reflects her lady at the prow
and all eyes together search for the New Moon

HEAVENLY DAYS

you look good pregnant.
all of a life
inside itself a geode
ultraviolet alone swells.
be a singer. Muslims

drop a stitch
to keep the cloth this side
of perfect. it'll come back
on you before you know it.
God don't sew.

better get better,
liberty.
you look good.
& now you go
resuscitate the air.

Adieu Mama Calypso
blow me a kiss straight home
beyond the jewel cave
across the purple wave
oars winnow.

Hello; hello.

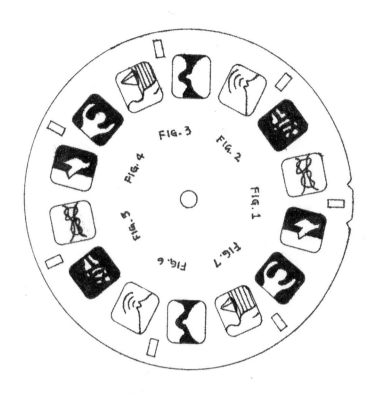

12 o'clock high

<u>the nether millstone</u>

they became what they beheld

men communicate only through their emanations

as a man is so he sees

distinguish the individual from his present state

---

behold   emanation

•

see   state

★
★
★
★
★

<u>the</u> <u>button</u>

> will be useful.
> it'll show up
> often in your dreams.

Reality is unfinished business or there would be no extent, and the time a man knows, comes to know when he stares, is what history enables him to confirm, that the extent is a limit.

—Charles Olson

⋆

<u>aether</u>

This air shineth night and day of
resplendour perpetual and is so clear
that if a man were abiding in that
part he should see all, one thing and
another and all there is, fro one end
to the other, all so lightly or more
as a man should do here beneath upon
the earth the only length of a foot
or less.

<u>a lens of air</u>

⋆

Thus is the heaven a vortex passd already, and the earth
A vortex not yet pass'd by the traveler thro' Eternity.

The <u>War</u> <u>of</u> <u>the</u> <u>Roses</u>

perspective looks through

times are contemporaneous in perspective,
everywhere at once.

the mathematical perspective of
Brunellesco, "vanishing point"

————the direction of the light————

Blake's "white dot for a center"
with <u>gyrations</u>
        /
(Steinmetz: gravitation: the
 centrifugal force of an
 imaginary velocity)
 /
materializes the human primate
horizontal scan perspective
establishing ratios according to
apparent outlines of natural objects
discovered by peripheral vision
(the eye is looking at nothing,
a "vanishing point"!) <u>macula</u> <u>lutea</u>

(<u>a Guinea</u>)

vanishing point perspective is based on the illusion that both eyes view a thing at once. the other eye is at the v.p., 'looking back'. Don Juan asked Castaneda which eye did he see his vision with.

". . . when two sounds are presented simultaneously to both ears, any verbal signals such as words, nonsense syllables, and even separate speech sounds are better discerned by the right ear and all other acoustical stimuli such as music and environmental noises are better recognized by the left ear."

             —Roman Jacobson

★
★
★
★

"94. The degree of genius is determined by its velocity, clearness, depth, simplicity, copiousness, extent of glance (COUP D'OEIL), and instantaneous intuition of the whole at once.

copiousness of glance"

       —WB, <u>Anno.</u> <u>Lavater</u>

<u>look in both my eyes at once</u> Marcia said

Viewmaster^{tm}

PERSPECTIVE: methodology

GAZE SCAN	FIXED SCAN	STARE
•	•	•
(scribble) particulars encountered	(perspective) particulars triangulated	(design) particulars delineated
•	•	•
touch surface	ear touch	EAR
paint	fresco balance	staind glass
	•	

shamanic bone vibes

1) gaze scan of vision across fixed scan on a visible object
2) fixed scan over stare
3) stare over gaze scan or vice versa

mapparama 360° horizontal round the man

Cézanne got it down so a twist of his head as much as a breath or a heartbeat moved it into a new place altogether.

SPIRITS ARE ORGANIZ'D MEN!

"In madness everything happens because
nothing can be seen in perspective."
                                    —Henri Michaux

PERSPECTIVE: situation

organization of the ground.
"landscaping" *vs* "projection"
(a portion of existence: "interior
decorating" / "the house is such a
mess" / "I'm so fat" &c)

projection organizes a perspective or
BACKGROUND for a thing and conceives
the thing the spirit of the ground

The Earth of Tomorrow, Four to Go:

Los was the fourth immortal starry one, & in the Earth
Of a bright Universe Empery attended day & night
Days & nights of revolving joy, Urthona was his name
In Eden; in the Auricular Nerves of Human life
Which is the Earth of Eden, he his emanations propagated

Earth gave the feet a hero's welcome
head in the clouds a birdseye view

•

things done & things said: the actions
get the words home. worlds are not
intermeasurable except as mapping . . .
dramatic principle: same thing done
same thing said.   *in the beginning*

•

Gothic cathedral musical asymmetric
human forms atop symmetrical bases.

•

second storey man

•

a juggler watches an x

•

"Since Perspective is but a Counterfeit of the Truth, the Painter is not oblig'd
to make it appear real when seen from Any part, but from One determinate
Point only." —Andrea Pozzo

•

Kepler: "I will indulge my sacred fury"

•

Perspectives are meanings of different distances for things removed.

•

The square root of minus one is called an *imaginary number* and not an *illusory number*, because it does not pretend to be something that it is not.

　　　　　　　　　　　　　　　　　　　　　　—M. Polanyi

•

STURM'S INTERVAL (Johann Christoph Sturm, 1635-1703). The distance between the anterior and posterior foci or focal points in the eye. (*Stedman's Med. Dict.*)

•

pre-perspective shows all (at least one side of all) figures: both legs of a mounted man, end-to-end instead of side-by-side-behind. perspective hides the way the world does. Ajanta.

•

put em up to cover their windows
cave men did, a horse over a bison
over a bear

inside or outside the frame <u>mystiche</u>
<u>landschaft</u> Persian miniatures, grass
laid flat along the stream, black silver
everything in place by color & outline
seen from inside. each proportion each
thing's own. no artificial subordination,
all paratactic & idealized, or great

Da Vinci: The secret of the art of drawing is to discover in each object the
way in which a certain flexuous line, which is, so to speak, its generating
axis, is directed through its whole extent.

•

<u>Horizontal Gravitation: Vanishing Point Earth</u>

the Elements substantial, the flexuous line has to be drawn to be seen by
any other; not material elements dark & light the vegetable eye records,
but Elements, that rise, fall, attract, repel, according to innate propensities
or loves: supernatural selection:

telekinesis————synchronicity

      Don Juan:
    "agreements"

    _____

       omens

    _____

SLALOM

a view interrupted by stations, fixations
or centers (*vs* foci of optics) whose stories
make up the time of the individual—what
happens to him, in the flesh, to name
and so make portable its origin, his life

the earth is so much larger locally than any
firmament. hands & eyes house, enclose,
immure. ears open to the traffic. the
acoustic nerve double, hears & balances

Time & Space are Real Beings a Male
& a Female Time is a Man Space is a Woman
& her Masculine Portion is Death.   —WB

•

teach: "to show how to do"—to penetrate
the Fear (of travelling: <u>errore</u>, wandering)

    Ockham, Mercator

      1 to 1

<u>I met a tree on Elmwood Ave.</u>

Kepler introduced the elliptical orbit into celestial mechanics
(2 foci: the sun is one)

QUANTA INTELLIGENDA

quantum mechanics: "a description of steady states in which there is no motion or else the state of motion does not change. Now and then, as we have seen, a jump occurs from one of these steady states to another."

—Sir James Jeans

Trobriand **pela,** to jump: their only connective

       ocular power & optical activity

     color & outline : enantiomorphy
   periphery & focus : corpus callosum

<u>Nature has no Outline</u> : <u>but Imagination has</u>.

     root & river sine curve down
     root hard river easily

     thigmotropic eyes (Kepler)
     horizontal (Ouranian) gravitation

     intensity, duende
          vs   / "white dot"
     vanishing point

•

     the only way (river, stretchmark
     _____

     no way   (one way, thigmotropic

        ROOT

       <u>anisotropy</u>

Generally speaking, red and yellow favour abduction, blue and green adduction. Now, on the whole, the significance of adduction is that the organism turns toward the stimulus and is attracted by the world—of abduction that it turns away from the stimulus and withdraws towards its center.

—M. Merleau-Ponty

starting in different bands and perhaps directions, the procession of daylight thru the spectrum ('image') thru the day within a blue cloud dome, also different for species, & of use for hunterly extensive savvy of the range.

a neolithic islander flown by whites new to him blindfolded in a copter, labyrinthine 50 miles flight off shore beyond landfall, only the big O horizon seen & dumped him in the 'water', swam in tight circles a spell, sniffing & sip sip. hauled aboard from where he'd never been before accurately reported his position. all systems go.

glued to the horizon couriers of ole Thibet made time with truckin' strides mile after mile over the mountain ice in Doppler strut. "Thus spoke FRATER PERDURABO as he leapt from rock to rock of the moraine without ever casting his eyes upon the ground."

the signs of age or of experience. presbyopia especially. 'good ears' (resonance of earth & sky; 8 cycles per second.

shakes his head
listening, no
can't see it yet
wait till I
see where it is

•

owls can't roll their eyes
they're fixed in their sockets
so they roll their heads
Athena
with Medusa at her breast

•

terrene

night falls in the desert
like a star

even at arms length
alongside you
closer for breath

mountains the far edge
might as well be rain

walk to walk fro
the hills move
undetected

banded stone
my galaxy came

Hope & Fear are—Vision

stand by. we've done praying.
1st message by telegraph
the joint
at Promontory Point
:Union Pacific

•

fruit let flower fall

tree let fruit

fire drew the rain

all we gave or wanted to

grew back again

•

looking-into-each-others-
eyes-each-wishing-the-other
would-do-what-both-desire-
but-are-incapable-of-doing

•

stance: the v of eyes
to center of gravity
upon the land. swung up.

portrait: the subject's
choice of clothes
within environs.

Generally speaking the weather conditions conducive to the greatest charm
are the very opposite of those which favour the view of a mountain peak
seen from below. In the latter case the emphatic form is best displayed by
the uniform background of blue sky. In the former, the best condition is
that of a blue and white sky in which the scale of the cloud pattern is of the
same order of magnitude as that of the land below.

—Vaughan Cornish

the principle of size constancy, that the tiny figure on the horizon is known
to be a giant, that what seems insignificant to others fills with wonder &
delight. faster than response, quicker than reception. inceptive creation.

the □ inch garden

in the acre field

•

Throughout history the landscapes of perception have been small. . . . The impressionists seldom went beyond a scale which could be taken in by a single focus. . . . The first modern landscapes were exceedingly small—only about three inches by two inches.

—Kenneth Clark

•

miniature < red (the pigment for

miniature focus (focus a hearth

<u>the red globule of blood</u>

a candle in the sunshine

A small-scale pattern can be appreciated as an ornamentation of the domi-
nant, large-scale pattern, but if these are placed side by side the eye has to
readjust its field of view.

—Vaughan Cornish

ocular power

optics: two vanishing points, one in each eye,
each 16th of a second or so, a glance chosen,
maintained in a stare by balance
(the other eye, the one not looking out,
looks in, is body indistinct from soul)

As a man is, so he sees

manners lead us to expect (habits set us up
to be surprised by) syntax, mapping out
projection following exactly into the new
new world, "a city on a hill" Winthrop said
standing on one, I imagine, too

•

where rainbows appear
depends on where
you're standing

The hall of the two truths

send the voice to the space behind the pupil

 1000 words a word

Jesus brushed the words away
of such authority
among adulterers

•

"Our Host" who occupies
the Center of the Cavalcade
(the Fun afterwards exhibited on
the road may be seen depicted
in his jolly face)
                —WB

•

well uh

resume the conversation after varying
absences at full energy as if no time
had elapsed between the conversants

The most sublime act is to set another before you

VISION

We live to see what comes before us.

I

A bobcat crossed the road at dusk.
Two little boys came past
carrying a pail with Nothing inside it.
The leaf shadows barely quiver on the ground.
The wind blows through the date palms.
A man rides a white mule back and forth
along a trail, and the rope he pulls from
his saddle horn draws up water from the well.

Day after day, step after step, I walk along some old-new ancient road.
While time, drifting with my footprints, drifts in the dust by my footprints
in that road. While the sun, dropping lower, circles the circling dancers. A
windmill just begins to spin on the horizon, the quiet evening comes in the
red sky and drops down onto the darkening earth. The knowledge not my
own, circling the fires around me, Indian women singing about rain, drums
beating in the smoky night, and the sparks go up and disappear. Tongues
of flame licking from some mouth in the wood, that howls up into the sur-
rounding darkness.

Or walking through a storm at night when suddenly lightning flashes
and shows clearly all that's around you, but after the light's gone you forget
the picture of the strange country it's shown you.
Your thoughts are made in electric and magnetic fields charged and
released by that lightning and those clouds given to your mind to think by
sun and wind.

One evening on an island, I left them, climbed up toward a mesa along a canyon of palm trees. Found a spring that flowed from some lava rocks, and a dove there drinking by the water. Ospreys perched on the tops of the saguaros, and I drank, and lay down and slept by the pool.

And there by that pool she came to me, softly, walking in the night, carrying a net of reata-like webbing I could hardly see at the edge of the pool in the light, dim light. The palm fronds clacked, and the tree frogs croaked while she lay beside me whispering, till I'd forgotten she'd come to me, then softly, softly, she led me away.

So in forgetting, again, she comes to me, softly, walking in the night, and brings me something I can't see, at the edge of a woods in the dim light. The fir limbs sway, and the pine limbs sway while she lies beside me whispering.

Night after night she came, and told me how she laid the moonlight along the slopes of the mountains, and dropped uneven shadows from the mesquite leaves onto the ground. And how she made the wind blow, so still I hardly knew it was there, but gently, gently blowing out of the South, blowing the limbs.

The leaves on the maples tremble softly on their long stems, and the trees turning red and yellow on the hill. The shadows of the leaves sway softly on the grass. The women and men you know, you do not know.

And so she came to me, though I can't remember where she's come from, or where she'll go when she leaves. But if she becomes all that is around you, hold to her and she will tell you who she is.

Her shadow lies like a ridge in the colors of the sun. Ring of ripples around her fingers, woman suspended in the shadows on the water, shadow of shadow on the rock, a bird calling across the grey ridges. Shapes of some hawk's wings glide in volcanic rock crescents from lips of the desert lava cone, bones by Volcan de Chichi lie in a crevice in the rock.

Once, I waited in a grove of aspen, light leaves above the earth quaking there in the wind, a dog ran over the tall mountain grasses. Aspen leaves and the sea, that I might go further . . . stages, that the Earth blows on our faces and hands. The body of the grass bending in the wind, when will she come back among the grey-barked trees? Cool and moving through the East side of the grove, above my head and gone.

II

I get up in the morning and carry out feed.
A heifer lopes away from the water trough
while her mother drinks, and lifts her head,
and glistening streams of her saliva
drift down onto the ground,
and the water-float bobs in the water-trough,
as she lowers, and lifts her head;
then runs away while I watch her.

Don't sell away the beauty of her body
and her eyes
            the shape of some wild deer drinking by the water
she lifts her head and sees you looking into her eyes, then runs off through
the glittering rocks by the stream, and time after time you look and try to
see her when the wind rustles through the leaves there where you think
she's gone to hide.

As though I've been taken to some place where the sunlight comes down
through the shadows in the trees, or where the light in the room suddenly
gets brighter to the right side of the fire place, and in that moment I seem
to know whoever it is who sits beside me in the darkness outside of the
windowpanes.

There stands a brown steer in the mid-day shadow by a dark rock, but
when I crossed to the other side of the arroyo and came to the rock where
he stood, he was gone. So I come to circle around that place, out through
the rocks, and arroyo sand and couldn't find a sign of him coming away.

So he lies there still in the shadow of the brown rock, through winter and the summers and the days.

"*Este se llama El Canyon del Diablo,*" Carlos says. A dust devil swirls past us like a sound of cool water rushing over rocks, and whirls on past up through the canyon, while a yellow wasp buzzes around the horse's head, and the bright conchos on the edges of my chaps, and a cactus wren warbles here among the ocotillo, and another answers on the canyon's other side. The East wind blows softly, blows, and blows.

The rippling in the water, or the blowing East wind, so the old mysteries in those voices go into our ears and into our voices, and from those old tongues of water and wind tell us how to come to know her messages echoing like Indian drum beats from the red cliff sides of her heart again. The clear rivers and blue lakes that run in her bloodstreams, her soft clothes of redwood trees and pines, to bring back the eagles and ospreys for our eyes to learn to see into the distances watching their wings float . . . far away into the years to come, far away into years past, into the clear blue sky.

And the palo verde seeds fall as my visions fall into ripples of her valleys and her mountains. A woman's lips, the open earth. Your soul becomes incarnate like a leaf that drops down into the water and drifts off on the stream.

Where the trail is so much gone
no one but my eyes
through the myrtle and ferns
with the lace works of light dropping
to the leaves.

Oh the shadows of the leaves
sway softly on the grass
and the women and men
you know you do not know.

III

THINKING IN THE EARTH'S MIND

turquoise stones in the creek bed, the sound
of the horses' hooves in the sand
her shadow lies like a ridge in the colors
of the sun

the color of her body is golden
darkness looks out from the caves of her eyes

the color of her body is golden in the lava
pools beneath the rock. Darkness looks out
from the caves of her eyes, a turtle swims
across the quiet water. Darkness watching
darkness in the cave orbits of each other's
eyes we look into

WINDS THAT BLOW IN THE MIDDLE OF HER SOUL

Freddy said, as we came over a pass into the Vermejo, meadows running off to the West, and snow on the bald peaks above the timber: "It's pretty rough country up here, this is where she says 'Let's see how good a man you are'."

And Alfredo dreamt that he and I were following a woman down out of the mountains when she disappeared walking ahead of us in the clear vega, and we lost her in this Vermejo country.

Slowly, slowly riding over the whiteness, elk tracks, and dropping on the snow, to hunt what cows and calves we've missed, gathering to ship at the Ring Place corals. Dally the split reins around the saddle horn, and stop by some green lichen rocks, while the clouds of light snow drift down from the fir limbs, and fall into the whiteness where a turkey's passed.

Earth's moods, and your moods, are the sunlight changing along the Sangre de Christos at morning and evening when the sun rises or goes down, or they say that the earth turns 'round, and the light of the sun and the Earth changes as she looks down deep into your eyes, past the circling flickers and habits of your eyes, down, down, into the dark centers she knows where you bring the sky for her seeds to grow into sky and the winds and the earth, and she brings you earth for your seeds to grow into the sky and the wind and the earth.

The cosmic weather of stars and planets swirling through empty space like grains of blowing sand, coming with the brightness of stars and planets across the black spaces of the breathing universe.

The flowing creeks of the earth and the rivers and winds have put her colors and notes into your eyes, into your body, into the rippling humors and streams of your mind. Her shapes and lines and colors, the sounds around you are telling you what you are and what to be.

The peeping of a robin with a stick in its mouth that flutters its wings and tail, perches on the wire by the locust tree, telling you what to do, how to narrow the flowing river that you are and cut deep into the earth like a canyon stream.

Wind, weather, water, have written the lines in the lips of the blowing sand, written the words I say to you now, written the rivers crossing the land, written the roads out of trails and grasses, written the lines in the palms of your hand.

So while earth dreams I walk inside her head, turning from side to side to talk with the people passing. And a man steps out from the market where I walk and sells fruit along the sidewalk. And the people pass, and the people pass, and stop to talk or buy or sell. While a woman in grey walks across the street, while I draw the coat together around me to cover my soul, like a woman who lifts her hands to cover her breasts when she looks out her window and sees the winter coming, and the slate colored sky above the lake, and listen to the sounds of the town in the leaves and the cars and the people passing.

You hold inside you all that goes away, so I walk by streams that have no end, or stand to wait on street corners in the sun . . . or stand listening for some wind that moans in the grasses around me. Her hair the color of fall swirling in the trees, a rock lying broken in the dirt, black dust from the sea's kelp weeds. It's all unreal to walk over the ground I knew so well. A quail calling from the yellow grass—no more than quail here, and tracks of mice in the sand.

So I've dreamt my dreams awake and they've washed me like the sea, and flowed about the ground I walked and fluttered like the leaves. And the time won't come again, or the words, or the motion of her arms thrown as stones into the water. Watch how the arms of the clock are turning and the bees buzzing in the ribs of the roof and the blue sky drifting beyond them.

Though you've forgotten who you were . . .
   though you've forgotten who you were
   when she told you her songs to sing,
though you've forgotten who you were
   who sang her songs to the air,
though you've forgotten who you were
   who could make her sing her songs,
though her arms ache for you and you want
   to come to her and you sit there
   waiting to hear her song,
the wind blows on past you over the ranges
   of blue mountains and carries her
   into the blue distances where
   your eyes can't see.

Oh thinking, feeling people:

    Laborers, presidents, blue collar workers,
    vice-presidents of governments and businesses,
    kids in blue jeans waiting out the summers,
    working in gas stations and cafes,
    smoking dope under the noses of the police,
    or screeching your tires on the roads,
    long-haired people living in lean-tos and old
    adobe houses spiritually resettling the land . . .

    bring to the children of the years to come
    that Indian vision of the Earth's old family
    Old vision of the white man we lost long ago
    that Homer tells was ours.

MESSAGES

THINKING OUT LOUD ABOUT MESSAGE

Sign is the stimulus for vision & message. What for me connotes worthwhile sign usually falls into the category of animal or natural, and usually the sign will reside in my mind over a period of time while it accumulates other signs—sort of like a magnet might draw metals to it. These signs combine to create a vision. In writing down the vision I will begin to consider the message to me, and whatever message the poem finally has is that message. How I make it work is not to talk about the message, but to relate the signs as they were—or as they fit into the final message. Often there are signs that don't enhance a particular message or vision, and these signs get lost somewhere along the way. In other words, you have in the final version a vision which generalizes itself into a message.

An instance of a sign: I might see a flock of crows flying in some particular direction. If there is no apparent reason for their flight, or for their direction, I will be aware of the phenomenon as sign. I won't know of what, but I'll carry the image until it multiplies into several images. If I've seen crows flying north, I will be tuned to north and anything out of the north or that relates to it in any way for me is likely to attach itself in my mind to the image of the crows. Finally the images will have congregated to the point that I'll have a sense of knowing something I didn't know before. I'll write them down and when I see them written they will generalize themselves into a meaning and that meaning becomes message and is different from any one sign. It might be inherent in the signs—will be—but is more than the signs themselves.

The natural relationships of animals and birds will obviously enter into the signs they give me. In other words, I am not laying out a message—it evolves from the stimulus. It evolves to a point where I sense its presence. I think nearly always I am hard put to tell you exactly what the message might be, but I think that the images which make me feel that I've gotten something from them will make others feel the same way. I think there is communication between things of an unlike nature. I think for instance that birds can communicate with people. Animals can and will communicate even more—especially wild animals. I think that places—configurations of rocks and trees and water in places—have at least auras which are meaningful. I don't think they're accidentally meaningful. Anything with aura has personae who come like the personae of persons you meet.

The sense of message comes from an awareness of personae and from the communication between the personae and yourself.

The nature of an animal or bird stays in his parts. The wings of a crow, the claws of an owl speak at least owlness and crowness. Pound said that a poet was the antenna of his race. I think that poetry has to deal with the gods—whatever gods there are. Good poetry is a message from the gods. If I see signs that come from nature—which are generally the only signs I personally see—the gods I'm concerned with are natural gods. (Maybe they're not gods, maybe they're spirits, maybe they're ghosts, maybe they were people but they're not people anymore but ghost people, or maybe they are people, people in some sort of frenzy that separates them from the usual or enhances the usual. It's these people that give messages.

Things fashioned by man from nature, or things made by man and worked on by nature have spirits. Anything has spirits if they're willing to let you know they're there.

When I begin a poem I'm looking for the message, what the spirits have to say to me. Once I have the sense of the message I can try to focus the message.

I see poetry as a celebration—a celebration of everything that exists, is alive, or has been alive (in all senses of the word). For me a good poem is one that has in it enough spirits that I know what's going on, what's being celebrated. I once saw a cow with a placenta still hanging from it, a calf lying on the ground beside the cow. All by themselves they were the celebration of birth. Above the cow and the calf there were crows and hawks circling. With death hanging over them the cow and calf became a celebration of the whole thing, the thin balance that life is.

I present what has shown itself to me, then acknowledge what I've found. I acknowledge signs and by presenting themselves they generalize, make a story, give a message, whatever story or message that these particular spirits want told or given. In a way it's as though I'm a door for the spirits to walk through, or a mouth for the spirits to talk through. I suppose you could say that my role as poet is little different than a naturalist's, except that he sees feathers or skins where I see spirits. I'm recording phenomena that appear to and through me. I don't really think that I have any message, but that the message gives itself through what has shown itself to me. I think that anything really considered a message has to come that way. If someone has something that they consciously want to tell someone else it won't come across in the same way. The poet gets in the way. The poet doesn't let the thing talk for itself. He comes with a preconceived idea and that's the idea he puts down. His idea is message and any images are there only to prove his point. It's all in how it comes through you. If you have a preconceived notion it won't work. You have to give the place, the spirits. They have to do their own talking. When someone tells you about something you're getting his idea of it, you don't know what he really saw. You have only the message he wanted to give. You have to give the spirits, not what you think about them.

Sometimes you can go on from all this. If the spirits are really with you and you know what it is they're saying, you can talk back, converse with them. This is the hardest thing to do, because you're likely to lose them and you won't have anything. But if you can get what they're saying, and if you can talk to them, and you're where they're at, you've gone as far as you need to go.

All through the night they rode
circled the Pole Star

blue white yellow & red ribbons
an iron bell before me

next to the cedar stood an oak
—the road ran between them—
I hung a rope from the oak, climbed it
could see more of the mountain—gold—in the north

the goat—Thunder—was killed at harvest
the dog ate her heart

we filled the room with hemp smoke—owl claws & feathers
outside, I looked into the dog's eyes
saw a dead man under the cedar

the blond woman came down from the mountains
watched over the child's birth

drunk, I pulled on a string of blue beads & iron bells
rung them—the bottom bell came off in my hand
I walked ahead, the road muddy in heavy rain
she followed, baby bundled in her arms
the wind louder than the rain where we came into the trees

where we'd watched for deer, along the river
the bell before me, a woman
crashed, killed herself
thrown from her car, her body under my truck

I found spotted mushrooms under the cedar

found a fox dead in the road—traded her skin
for the spotted feather of a golden eagle

with blue white yellow & red ribbons
I tied three sheep skulls high in the oak
at dusk with iron pots for drums
I sang a circle around the house & down the road

at midnight—the roar of a single motorcycle
then another & another—thirteen riders
beer to fill the bed of a truck
we sang, ran berserk, raced
all night over the dark hills—into & out of the flames
the best rider of them all fell into the coals
we pulled him out—unburned—put him to bed
he slept until dusk, was the last to leave

the child grew, one summer night squealed for joy
the iron pots rang where they hung
& the riders came again
burned their fire, all of the wood
in the morning one of them pierced the child's ears

when we left the place, he had returned
stood with the others in the road, waved after us

rounding a curve, far to the east
a golden eagle flew up before us

ANALYTIC PSYCHOLOGY

"the soluble forest is swimming across"

for Harvey Brown

and the angel of the Moon

Wander as you will, take every turning, you can't
find out the psyche's limits; so deep is the bathos of its
logos, so high the byss of its abyss.
—HERACLITUS (*frag. 45, modified*)

your own discourse is the other's unconscious,
                      or
this bardoplane is god's ignoring,
          her own backside.
—J. NACAL

I

a "technical study"
tracking the Numbers
given the River Map
and the Riverine Words

      a "technical study":
           Complex Psychology
           Analytic   "
           Archetypal   "

                     :

        the game of Carl Gustav Jung

that naming
      is gaming

II

who gauges the shadow games?

I reek I reek
of *mimologique*

★

inaccessible Perfume

Aromatherapy
you *logophiliques*

lying in shadowy leaves
of the floating tree!
His hair. And her.
Ophelia-tree, ophidian crossed!
The shadow was lost
till we found it in play.

III

in the blazing stadium
        of mirroring thirds

the word of the law
        is liberty, a book:

    liber   – – – legis

a writ is a route.

IV

A WRIT is a route, a way and the map of a way.
It figures and we make of it our figure, you make of it your
figure, I make it of mine. It is mind, and no mind, inner
and dinner and outer and doubter.

Doubtless these figures are crystal.

From the center of nothing something spreads out,
that then there now. From zero jumps two, two being how
something is apprehended. Only a stone's throw from writing
to root. The rite of winter is the root of spring.

The house stands on its cellar and grows up. Also
grows down from its garret invisibly, as the crown of a tree
flourishes the idea of its root.

Shine, heaven, darken and shine, that the process
may stir as things emerge from the void of no-thing. It is
plenty. All around us the letters are cast, to be spelt, to
be sown like spelt, grain of the garment unseen as green as
it makes it.

Do you, do I?

V

Spelt from the mummy's tomb:
                    a cereal poem:

    it die and be
    it comes as it goes

        Eleusinian

VI

the   Poem
        comes in its own cocklight,
time the solary flowering bird sings up the rising god

He-Who-Comes

di-wo-nu-so-yo   Zagreus

Him-at-Home-in-the-Depths-of-the-Sea

———————————————

"Neglect not the Dawn-Meditation"

AUMGN

VII

in light of inscribing

To say that life ends in
the violet light
of the straw-bottomed chair
is to begin at the end:
where to start out from:
starting out from light,
first breath, first light,
out of the mothering hole
burrow of blood, membranes
flowering rich red,
pulsating, pulsating,
is to ask why start?

start because we *were* started
spinning-tops of desire
not disorder ending in vulgar order,
death,
not either,
rather,
neither nor.

This chair
        charily goes
in the light of this chair
        by flesh inscribed it is,
this hand,
        this chair the pen I hold

in the violet light of
the straw-bottomed chair
that has swallowed the shadows of green and the shadows of red

VIII

psyche inscribed in biohologram:

locating in time is always first step
and first error is separating
"environment" from its "going-on-in"

•

"the very act of
        and the intention behind
                        observing

                disturbs the observed"*

supraliminal language-field is body-field
            is feeling
                    and feeding:

electromagnetic you   Nu-it.

                        Anagnorisis.

*Lawrence Beyman, "Quantum Physics & Paranormal Events", in *Future Science*, Ed. John White.

Schrödinger's cat is out of its box,
lying in wait for the mouse in the basement:
what's unbeknownst to us is somewhere beknownst:
Swedenborg stoops to stroke Schrödinger's cat.

•

so I am always finding in feeling
locating in shifting
the terms that compose me
the rhetorical cinnabar lode
whose clavicle's wavicle's key..

IX

in exopsychology
the messenger substance
figures as figure,
young bitch and old maid,
the boy in the sun,
old man harboring babe,
etc. etc.
all decans and images thereof.

Light speaks the tongue of the shadow.
Others' dreaming invades our sleep.

On the genetic clavier
the genie decodes

"always remaining subject"

        and the subject's discourse
                is the others' unconscious.

X

       on the wheel
          the buckets communicate,

   the gold is poured from one to another, from her to us to me

   to him to them and under the greenwood tree

     the proud shifters prance.

       Dusk, and
          the gate of the tongue is opened,
            the tinctures cross,

   and tomorrow rustles in yesterday's corpse.

    Light the death lamps, see the shadows condense!

Bahlasti! the dust settles
          and the figures uprise.

XI

So the river rites are done
     and eleven signifies

     sinless and of us
      of what traces us
       and races throughout

not two, not one, not none

           of us,

     and Her again.

OF SIGNIFYING STONES

There are four philosophic stones Elias Ashmole writes of, in his Prolegomena to his anthology *Theatrum Chemicum Brittanicum*, the Stone Minerall, the Vegitable, the Magicall, and the Angelicall:

1. the Minerall "the which is wrought up to the degree onely that hath the power of Transmuting any Imperfect Earthy Matter into its utmost degree of Perfection"

2. ". . . by the Vegitable may be perfectly known the Nature of Man, Beasts, Foules, Fishes, together with all kinds of Trees, Plants, Flowers, etc. and how to produce and make them Grow, Flourish, and beare Fruit; how to encrease them in Colour and Smell, and when and where we please, and all this not onely at an instant, Experimenti gratis, but Daily, Monethly, Yearly, at any Time, at any Season; yea, in the depth of winter."

Of the Vegitable Stone "the Masculine part of it . . . is wrought up to a Solar Quality, and through its exceeding Heate will burne up and destroy any Creature, Plant etc. That which is Lunar and Feminine (if immediately applyed) will mitigate it with its extreme Cold; and in the manner the Lunar Quality benums and congeals any Animall, etc., unlesse it be presently helped and resolved by that of the Sun; For though they both are made out of one Natural Substance: yet in working they have contrary Qualities: neverthelesse there is such a natural Assistance between them, that what the one canot doe, the other both can, and will perform.

Nor are their inward Vertues more than their outward Beauties; for the

Solar part is of so resplendent, transparent Lustre, that the Eye of Man is scarce able to indure it; and if the Lunar part be expos'd abroad on a dark Night, Birds will repaire to (and circulate about) it, as a Fly round a Candle, and submit themselves to the Captivity of the Hand: And this invites mee to believe, that the Stone which the ancient Hermet (being then 140 Years old) tooke out of the Wall in his Cell, and shewed Cornelius Gallus, Ann. 1602. was of the Nature of this Vegitable Stone: For (upon the opening his Golden Box wherein it was inclosed) it dilated its Beames all over the Roome, and that with so great Splendor, that it overcame the Light that was kindled therein; Besides the Hermet refused to project it upon Metall (as being unworthy of it) but made his Experiment upon Veronica and Rue.

3. By the Magicall or Prospective Stone it is possible to discover any Person in what part of the World soever, although never so secretly concealed or hid; in Chambers, Closets or Caverns of the Earth: For there it makes a strict Inquisition. In a Word, it fairely presents to your view even the whole World, wherein to behold heare, or see your Desire. Nay more, It enables Man to understand the Language of the Creatures, as the Chirping of Birds, Lowing of Beasts, etc. To convey a Spirit into an Image, which by Observing the Infleence of Heavenly Bodies, shall become a true Oracle: And yet this as E.A. assures you, it is not any wayes Necromenticall, or Devilish; but easy, wonderous easy, Naturall and Honest.

4. "Lastly, as touching the angellical Stone, it is so subtill, saith the aforesaid Author, that it can neither be seene. felt. or weighed but Tasted only. The voyce of Man (which bears some proportion to these subtill properties,) comes short in comparison; Nay the Air it selfe is not so penetrable, and yes (Oh mysterious Wonder!) A Stone, that will lodge in the Fire to Eternity without being prejudiced. It hath a Divine Power, Celestiall, and Invisible, above the rest; and endowes the possessor with Divine Gifts. It

affords the Apparition of Angells, and gives a power of conversing with them, by Dreames and Revelations, nor dare any Evill Spirit approach the Place where it lodgeth. Because it is a Quintessence wherein there is no corruptible Thing: and where the Elements are not corrupt, no Devill can stay or abide.

S. Dunston calls it the Food of Angels, and by others it is termed The Heavenly Viaticum; The Tree of Life; and is undoubtedly (next under GOD) the true Alchochodon, or Giver of Years; for by it Mans Body is preserved from Corruption, being thereby inabled to live a long time without Foode: nay 'tis made a question whether any Man can Dye that uses it."

XIII

        Signifying is butterfly catastrophe

between terminals of certainty, tall terminals
or virtues of the text, procedure a division,
under lilt of waves,
to register is to note the uniform:
this "uniform that music wears when most . . .",
such catch in the throat or eye,
a hit at dawn.
               Old and new dependencies, good harbor,
deserted beach of seaweed brown
I walk, distinguishing processes and systems . . .
       mouth is dry to speak a love,
       partition of the waves without exhaustion,
       blue accordion.

The sky black with derivates I only mumble,
the feelings beam, include a solitude
whose love pores over tables endlessly:
of action, tablature, guitar, and love
            a music pricked on vanishing.
On Eastern Point and in my head a tree of monarchs
          pullulates
   late butterfly catastrophe .

XIV

THE VEIL, and Making the Soul

                                    in American Numbers

        Sister perturbation:

        American desiring – tubes
sucking in phones and *klactoveedsedsteenotonique*
        for archetypal daedalion.

                so its Poets (Hers)
                        deal tedium
                unless
                                the Angel of Bethesda
                nods
                *****

        and not misheard
        and springs to life
        the time of Cotton Mather
        and Hart Crane

                stirring the pool – – *vibhakti*

the clutch at
        real hair

        (In England there was no sacred veil
                                to go behind)
here, the inelegant poem,
        hardly time to speak

                of Psyche's chores
        or even drag.

XV

GOD IN HIS IGNORANCE IS THE FATHER OF LIES

justify the domination by untruth, it does, the ugly myth:
                    by untruth the juice that stupefies
                    by untruth the cruel barbers' fantasies
                    by untruth the cellophanes enshrouding love
                    by untruth the dummies
                    by untruth the blinded horse
                    by untruth your hands chopping my blocks of
                          heart for so much bloody stew meat
                    by untruth the whispering handkerchiefs of torturers
          he kisses her under the untrue sign of festival
          he stabs her stabs him stabs their self in riddling stabs
          as what's corruption but that which mystifies
          as it shines undead
          not the mystery or bliss or satisfaction new in gasping overlaps.

to shun,
that is the mission of untruth,
to turn away,
to not attend,
handling the unhanded, down,
the hindrances,
the human sink, the cold and fading colors in, the greasy situation

    bottomless.

XVI

towery between . . . .

and flowers falling . . . .

every time I come this way . . . .

the endless . . . .

the work to dissolve

the news of the day in the news of the night

XVII

HERMES BIRD

Something is roosting in the hemlock boughs, visible
glittering behind the snow, sun rippling in frozen puddles. It
is feathered, it roosts, I see the flash of its eyes, it is alert,
a many-colored bird.

It is my zest, making ready there in the green and white tree,
ready to move the season a half-turn, turning what was, now
nothing, to something else, the pride of surprise unravished
by sunset.

Urgency flutters, the capable bird, lithe agency of glory. The
flush of the bird dominates the tree, making it background. The
bird can take off, at any time. It brings news from nowhere
to nowhere. It is unseizable. Wait till it sings.!

XVIII

is the number 18

the tablets are empty

everybody's crossed over

and no one has ever gone over

because always is never because

utterly utterly gone

and under the moon

the swimming forest dissolves

PHENOMENOLOGICAL

In February of 1985 I traveled with Donald Guravich and Diana Middle-ton-McQuaid, our neighbor in Bolinas, to the Yucatan Peninsula to visit the pyramids of antiquity and to acquaint ourselves with its contemporary culture.

My dear friend of many years, Bill McNeill, was in the hospital suffering from the last terminal stage of his illness. Bill, painter, poet, and student at Black Mountain College when Charles Olson was teaching there, knew he would not live much longer. We made an agreement that we would somehow 'meet' down there, 'between the real and the apparent.' This is a record of that journey . . .

February 14, 1984

          Tuesday 10PM Bolinas
       Looks like we're ready
      And now to bed.

February 15
           Just sitting down
   at cafe in front of the Hotel Caribe
First time alive in evening Merida.
        Cervezas on top terrace
Romantic full moon accompanied by frenzied
         jack hammers
drowning out conversation.
       Diana loses her bag
            (with everything in it)
but finds it back by the table
        We all vow to be more
Careful.

February 16
        Merida *is* hot and muggy and full
of rushing cars. We're still trying to find
the 'right' hotel room, price and all.
       300,000 inhabitants.
Our room has an overhead fan which Donald
and I bend to walk under—looks decapitating.
I make notes—5:30PM 160 pesos to the dollar.

The Mexico City newspaper says Ethel Merman
has died.

        Going to Santa Lucia Park to hear
a poet lady we see 'the government' pressing
into a new white columned building next to an
old stone cathedral. Everybody is dressed in
white short sleeved shirts. We think they
look like dentists.

> full Moon
> thru Acacia
> Merida
> Music
>   —Santa Lucia Park

February 18

    I notice a pretty girl tripping and
falling and it's Sara! with Joe. Back from
Palenque and right on time! We all go
On the Town and have two lunches and one
dinner.

February 19

        The four of us meet in Progreso,
the port town on the Gulf 20 miles away,
and drink rum and fresh coconut milk on the

beach, stretching out and looking around.

Is this a good place to stay
for a while? A German man who has the well
muscled legs of a walker gives us the name
of a good hotel here, with a proprietor who
speaks English.

February 20

Note to Bill McNeill
from Miss Kids.

Me, I just sit in my place
by the newly laid shrine
on blue bandana with banana
and Monte Alban Mezcal really early
from noon now 2 o'clock chat chat.

Waiting thru purple bougainvillea
blue cloud sky windy afternoon I feel

for Bill's new birth.

My phenomenology waits.
'The wrath of Juana' and tears from colonial
times in Mexico, Juana Ines de Asbaje, the
great poet.

Born of a Spanish father and a
Creole mother in the middle 1600s near
Popocatepetl she is the first truly Mexican

poet of New Spain, blending the Old World
and the New.

In her miracle play, *The Divine
Narcissus*, she argues that the sacrifice
of the Mexican corn god, and the ritual in
which his image shaped in corn dough is
eaten, anticipates the Christian symbolism
of the death and resurrection of Christ and
the Sacrament of Communion. This idea which
favors the native Indians was a big no-no
to the Catholic Church. She struggles thru
her life with compassion and talent in
intellectual pursuits, not granted to women.
'I began studying grammar, and my eager-
ness was so intense that I cut off four or
five inches of my hair, which is a natural
adornment on women.

I measured how far it had reached before,
and made a rule that if it grew that much
again before I knew some particular thing
which I had determined to learn while it was
growing, I would have to cut it again as a
punishment for my stupidity . . .

for it did not seem to me reasonable that a
head should be clothed in hair and naked in
knowledge, which would have been a more be-
coming adornment.'

She becomes a nun, but runs into trouble
with her mind. 'I thought to flee from myself
                    but wretch that I am
                    I took myself with me.'

She writes many many poems, but the Bishop
tells her it's all anti-Christian vanity
and takes away her books and papers. She
dies nursing plague victims at the age of
43 on April 17, 1695.

            Her poem "To A Linnet"
tells the story of this little bird who gets
eaten by a hawk for breakfast:

    Sweetest linnet, mournful little wing;
    scarcely had he seen the enchanted dawn
    than, at the first full throttle of a tune
    he discovered death, and lost his song.

February 21, Tuesday

        At Uxmal, 8:30 AM, in front of the Pyramid
of the Magician.
                    The sky is filled
with swallows catching early morning breakfast.

Everyone zoops up the impossibly steep steps
                    to the top and Don does too—

and now he is down again in a fine mist
of appearance.

As legend has it, this pyramid, Adivino
            was constructed
        by a dwarf with supernatural powers.

The temple's now inhabited by swallows, iguanas.
A black bird with scarlet-orange wing
                        and head markings.

    At the Temple of the Phallus
    Quietly 11:15 with my Japanese fan

The jungle here indeed exotic: ferns, cactus
    gumbo limbo, bromiliads, mimosa, and gold
flowers on dark unleafed branches

Chac gives us some afternoon rain and we wait
                in the Temple of the Turtles
And under a spreading tree.

February 23, Thursday

    We are on the way to Dzibilchaltun, a very
    large and very partially restored site of
    approximately 20 square miles, occupied
    continuously from 1000 BC until the Spanish
    conquest. Dzibilchaltun means 'where there
    is writing on flat rocks.'

2PM in front of the 'Temple of the Dolls'
with its most peculiar restoration which
plops in two front windows.
                              On a most
fortunately overcast day which shields us
from the heat. A large cenote near the
entrance continues a long way underground.
Supposedly all the large cenotes in the
Yucatan mysteriously connect up underground.

Iridescent green snakes in that scrub won't
kill you, but they'll make you very sick,
says fat American lady carrying a stick.

February 24, Friday

            Reading *Serenade* by James M. Cain,
a fast moving classic, which has the famous
iguana stew recipe. And worry about my funky
wardrobe falling apart.

T-shirt on bearded gringo in Progreso:
    'Kill everyone and let God figure it out.'
Skull, crossbones and green beret float under
that slogan.

February 25, Saturday

  I read Olson's *Mayan Letters*
and fall asleep. We all go to a funky cantina
and have a beer and some very strange little
snacks made from intestines and beets.

Returning to the hotel we prepare for Sara's
going away party, by drinking tequilla
and soda water. Several hours later and about
the time I am explaining the meaning of
religion to Sara, Donald announces that the
room is 'borracho.' His voice sounds very
clear and illuminated. We are all vastly
amused at our condition and carefully go out
into the night for supper at The Rodeo, a
small place decorated in American Cowboy
style, with a big poster of Tonto.

February 26, Sunday

And everyone looks a bit wan this morning
on the beach . . . We've moved downstairs to a
normal room which doesn't look like a good
idea from Bucky Fuller. I finish rereading
Mayan Letters and muse about the Yucatan 30
years ago, when Olson was here. So much
emptier, no big tours from Florida.

Sara packs and leaves for Merida. Anxious
today, a little inferma, Bill McNeill?

Dreams last night were hideous nightmares in
which I am evil murderer. I kill three or
four people. All the negative aspects
demonically crowding to the fore.

February 27, Monday

And what nightmare dreams last night again—
enough to wake me up I am so awful. All
these mad, bad dreams are destroying! I
must take refuge!
                    Returning to sleep I
dream I am at Dotty and Ray's where I am
using their typewriter on the bottom shelf
in the kitchen as a little toilet. Dotty
has shouted at me from the dinner table
about the planning commission meetings. She
is very angry at me.

                    Talking to Ed Dorn
who is speaking of brevity and directness—a
nearby critic points to his cynical direction.

Small groins off Bolinas Beach. Gwenn Spangler
in front of new glassed-in beach eating
establishment has nervous breakdown. The

Coastal Commission has obviously been paid off
to allow this. White linen tablecloths.
A salad is being served to an elegant black
couple. 'Look how sloppy it is' she says
critically 'the watercress is falling off
the plate.' The new partners, a young man
and woman, are very direct and energetic.
What's to become of Bolinas?

Early morning coffee, glad to be rid of dreams,
followed by walk on beach to west of Progreso's
mile long pier, picking up shells for Art
Okamura's birthday. We see rushing
clouds come in from the gulf to cover
the sun and it rains while we pack to
return to Merida.

February 28, Tuesday

To go to Chichen Itza. First read about
in Richard Haliburton's book in Upper
Darby Pennsylvania Junior High School 1940s
when he jumps in the Sacrificial Pool and
is knocked deaf and dumb for three days.

The first class bus is very comfortable
behind the driver's seat and we cruise
there in two hours.

The site was brought to world focus when
visited in the early 1800s by John Stephens
and Frederick Catherwood. Edward Thompson,
U.S. Consul to the Yucatan and an archaeologist,
at one time was the sole owner of the entire
site, reportedly bought for $75. He does
excavations there from 1895–1920 and dredges
the Sacrificial Pool finding many gold objects
and bones of women and children.

Sylvanus Morley and Eric Thompson
convince the Carnegie Institute and the
Mexican Government to restore some of the
ruins from 1924–1937, labor coming from the
Mayan Chamkom.

These temples were classic
Mayan until about 889 and then the 'Barbaric
Toltec Splendor' of the Itzas arrive to take
over.

The day is very windy and cold. Thou-
sands of tourists from all over the world
unload from buses for a quick tour.

It starts to become hilarious. People with
their comments in many languages. An
elderly German couple: 'The pyramids in
Egypt are much better.'

Constant flow up and down
    Kukulcan's Pyramid
A norte blowing and Don blowing
      his nose.

Like a human karma chain
   with U.S. help in restoring
this greatest of Mayan Toltec attractions
   Teenagers of U.S. galloping
up and down on
      history's past conquests.

I immediately challenge myself to El
Castillo's top.

And once there, weak legged, wind blowing
terrified to walk around the temple at the
top for fear I'll fall off

want immediately to descend while I can. What
vertigo! Holding on to the chain, praying
and trembling I descend backwards down the
narrow steps, remember the human sacrifice
practiced by the Itzas.

I have rubber legs for the next four days.

  The Sacrificial Well is crowded with tourists.
Plunk!

We sit down at a refreshment stand and write
a postcard to Gin John.

At the Platform of the Jaguars and Eagles,
stone carvings of the famous eagle with heart
in his talons, and jaguar with heart in his
claws, and on top of the hearts, a flower.

  Treading softly behind the Nunnery
  In old Chichen Itza
  I meet Leslie Scalapino

Blue and white flowered dress and webbed plastic
shoes, she's flying with friend Tom for
four days before she flies to Bard in New York
for readings. I tell her to say hello to
Alice Notley and Anne Waldman.

Returning to Casa Bowen we have early bed
and easy fiction.

March 5, Monday

  Means waiting from 1PM to 11PM hanging
  out in Merida until our train leaves for
  Palenque. Spent in the Cafe Express,
  the Zocalo, Hotel Caribe courtyard, Los
  Alemendros the great Yucatecan restaurant,
  and finally the train waiting station with

a romantic novel set in the last century
China and England with oodles of jewels and
costumes and affluence.

Our sleeping compartment, an old American
Pullman, is very self contained with sink,
toilet, undrinkable water, a nicely made
pulldown bed, and no springs! Do we ever
bounce thru the night!

March 6, Tuesday

      Morning on the train,
with service of hot coffee. A herd of
white cattle, countryside thatched cottages.
Across the aisle from Bob and Andrea from
North Carolina.
      Early morning dream has
Lucy Rose taking Nancy and Dotty and I on
a special ride to the Bolinas Beach in her
Volkswagon Bug—right on to the sand.

And we board a ferry boat and arrive in North
Carolina. She's a little worried that her
charge card maybe won't cover it all, but we
are her guests over there in the river woods

black faces pressing to the window. She has
a new baby with red hair—how did that
happen Lucy?

I try to call Bill McNeill's
mother who lives there, but remember she has
died, even tho I see her face.

       —Little Villages and rolling hills
on the way to Palenque.

    12:40 PM

At Palenque now, having visited
the Amazing Temple of the Foliated Cross
    in all its flowering fecundity—
etched on stone in the back wall panel
    is the Young Corn God.
        Donald is striding around
and blowing his nose, while I envy
    his agile enjoyment
        of this green mist beauty.

Well True Confessions Teenage History
    No Artist. No Personality.

Proud gorgeous history
    of Amnesia fat fellows

Little Releases in time-space
    personal to all, I suppose, and where
are the iridescent beetles.

This afternoon the attendant
with his peaked cap at the Temple of the Sun
is studying some lessons
when the Germans shake
the lemon tree vigorously at the entrance
of the path into the jungle
So white fragrant blossoms fall
to the ground
He jumps to his feet
and blows his whistle sharply.
They wave their hands, shouting
merrily and go in.

(I can't figure out his motives for blowing
the whistle on those loud souls.
Don't shake the trees?)

March 7, Wednesday

The great ruler Pacal is buried
in the Temple of the Inscriptions. He ruled
from 615 - 683 AD and died in his eighties.
His tomb with its grand sarcophagus was
discovered in 1956.

It is raining.
We have our straw hats
and our plastic capes.

We have gone
to the top of the Temple
of Inscriptions and down
to the Tomb of the Great Ruler
Pacal.
I am making a place
in the doorway of the Jaguar
Temple in the jungle.
A river runs below
the foot of this place
and the trees and vines
are deep and lush and green.

Monstera, bird's nest fern,
bromiliad, ceiba tree, and an arm
thick vine reflect my attempt
to display them
in the form of this body watching
The Temple behind
my back
The room in which I sit
flashes gold
thru the satiny silver air

And the iridescent blue
Butterfly is folded
up today under umbrella leaf

The room is reflecting
Looking thru this mind

Listening, tidying up, seeing
Top rustle of leaves as big snake
Rushes down to the stream
                              in rain time.

Don has walked to the top of the jungle ridge
to a clearing and a little settlement of
Mayans. 'What are *you* doing here?'
'Well, I'm a Botanist.'

        Seated by the side of the Count's
        Temple fourteen toucans
        fly by black in grey sky and

    Black head, white eye band
    Chestnut back, gold chest
            Insect catcher

A real Meditation Temple Garden

As we get ready to board the jitney back
to town five o'clock closing time, an
American camper truck pulls up and a
pleasantly plump white haired lady
jumps out asking excitedly
              'Where are we!
    What's the *name* of this place!'

March 8, Thursday

Morning

<u>Temple of the Cross</u>

The Guardian of the Temple is a Butterfly
we call the Ambassador

The Ambassador greets us
sits on my hand
then Don's where he stays
while Don takes several pictures
of it on his finger with
Sun Temple backdrop.
Eats a grain of sugar from sweet bun
gets its proboscis stuck and goes
sugar stoned for a while

A wonderful jeweled ornament on the light
straw hat, on the very finger
that writes this now.

The continuing embellishment
of Life in this ancient
Epitome of grace
Our eyes are blown up

Long human calls
away in the jungle
repeated over and over dying
wails, mournful,
elder

And then the Germans
come loudly taking over
        the territory and enter into
the jungle path, their voices
first muted by
the trees make loud sound to cover
            their unfamiliarity to
        keep together a noisy
assertive bevy.

            Then friend butterfly
is back in brown and red and yellow
            the most beautiful guard
of this Temple.

Get in line for tickets at 9 PM. We don't
get the last of the pullman reservations
because of those 'pushy' Germans and are
content with First Class Especial.
Except that Don looks grumpy and tired
sitting on train platform in straw cowboy
hat since the train doesn't arrive until
11:30. Lucky me
with an adventure book.

March 9, Friday

Morning 6:30 AM

Coffee comes thru and we have survived the
night! This is first class *especial* and
you've *got* to have the air conditioning on,
and it's insanely *freezing!* We put every
piece of clothing with us on, and wrap
our rain plastic over us, and try to drowse
thru the night.

      The rural countryside,
thatched roofs of palm, little piggies
under freight trains permanently stopped.

      Dreaming about Ebbe and Don as I awake—
who have just made love to this lady—
    A great and profound experience says Don.
'Nothing,' thumbs down, says Ebbe.

      And so goes the world
and beautiful memories
            of Palenque
    living ruins
   lichen growing walls
          always another
  turn brings
perfect vista

March 12, Monday

      Wake early, have coffee, and get bus
to Chixulub, 3 miles east of Progreso on
this Yucatan coast. Mile after mile of
fancy empty beach houses. Two beautiful
wooden galleons under construction for
lagoon tours somewhere.
                A few miles on
we find an empty sandy place to sit down
for a while on this hot sunny day.

    <u>She-shi Chixulub</u>

Bright white sand
     Dark blue sky
Thin band of blue
     green
    aqua marine
On horizon
      & light green
    olive stretches
Soft low waves
       at our feet are white
And long white streaks
    in the sky.

'I bet Larry Eigner
       would like it here'

and Bob Grenier
and Kathleen too for this day
at *this* beach.

Just let that gold butterfly
wing from Palenque fly away from notebook
pages down Chixulub Beach.
Walking back to town along the road,
a few peeks at lovely thatched roofed houses
tucked in coconut groves, stick fences,
white sand ground, swept all around.

Grand architectural mansions,
cement bungalows. Development on its way.

March 15, Thursday

Isla Mujeres

At Merida bus station waiting for
7 o'clock bus to Cancun. Rising at 4:10
with dreams of broken down Mexican courtyard
and building at night. Two kittens keep
getting tied up to be in front of firing
squad which consists of Duncan McNaughton
and Jon Bradley.
    —Firing squad for the kitties.

Keep memory compassionate of all the
   interconnections of people one has loved
and known.

March 16, Friday

       At Garrafon Reef
      swimming with mask and snorkel
   and fins on coral reef in clear
     glass like water to see
    gold and black striped fish
  flit by.

        We find
  our own little niche of sand
  and coral amid the masses of snorkelers
   on this tiny famous reef.

      Tour boats from
Cancun empty and load up Americans for a stop
I see an avenue of 30 swimmers go by . . .

     Charles! Use some
  imagination . . .
    Well it's hard to have imagination
   when you're getting so many
 first impressions

Our Lampara de Mesa
    Lampshade is a conch shell

The island is littered
    with caracole shell, must be
no protection for them

Little streets of toy town Isla
     sand and brick
teeny boutiques, & homes with T.V.
    sets and hammocks

Super torta from happy
    young lady in lime green hole
in the wall.

We sit in two chairs on the empty
   roof top and view the moon and town
all so close together

Very few cars on Isla Mujeres, mostly
motor bikes and bicycles.

      6 PM in our Room—
Reviewing this early morning's dreams . . .

In Memoriam for John Wieners

A beautiful inner atrium rotunda domed room
          with Steuben & Art Deco glass
on tall stands in shades of green,
          white walls, His favorite things
—A fitting memory, says a visitor.

     In the hotel across the street
      like a hymn the gringos sing
     Happy Birthday Dear Karen
          with its dying falls and harmonies
     Happy Birthday to You.

Bill's room: Bright, Cheerful
     with plants. The great Japanese
          flower arrangements.
The Stud. The Ambush. The studios.
     I'll be keeping care
          of your memory

No, you are not free
          from the memories
                of others, Ted Berrigan . . .

Jeannie Maxey shows me a pin
          of dove wings
               she will copy into a design
     for a book cover
          for a young boy who has died—

So sad. Write something
for his book.

March 17, Saturday

   The remains of the little Mayan temple
to Ixchel, moon goddess
            this morning in the rain—
      a dramatic perch on the southernmost
end of the island.
                  The taxi driver
   stops on the way to pick up a knife
on the road.

   Full moon rose 7:30 irregular
         orange behind cloud
   confused with horizon lights
      becomes dramatic red gold vehicle
   for Sun's reflection, rising swiftly

March 18, Sunday

   Like the past two mornings we have
heuvos rancheros (always different) and
coffee beside the tiny mercado of Isla.

Our last stroll along the island's
          windward side, we found some sun glasses,
just fine for Don, made in Korea.
                    When we board
the 10 o'clock ferry for the mainland I see
Orientals, so I make Don take his glasses off,
in case they're Koreans who will say,
   'What are you doing wearing my sun glasses!'

The bus to Merida hurls along the road
past the cunningly thatched Mayan houses,
with sweet little doors—walls of sticks
neatly lined up, stone or white plaster,
set in palm groves; chickens, pigs, little
gardens; and Mayan ladies in white skirts
and overblouses embroidered round the neck.
Long dark hair never cut. Rebozos always
with woven flecks of white.

    Arriving in Merida all the markets
and shops are closed up tight with streets
empty of the usual busy press of people
and vendors.
                    Until we reach the Zocalo
with Sunday strollers and buy the English
Mexico City News. Board the bus to Progreso
and get a little plastic bubble room
at the Miral Mar—everyone is at the Beach
today out here.

Muchos Gentes.
                    Diana is out visiting
on a boat nearby for dinner, leaving a note.

            She gets back after eight, & I wake
        up and go to her room to read
    the letter from Sara saying Bill died
                the Morning of March 10,
    in his sleep.
                    Go out with the dream.
    A sweet and generous gentleman.

March 19, Monday

                    Running parallel thoughts over
        Bill's last days and ours in Palenque—
            the Butterfly Guardian,
                        transcendental clarity

    A visit to a new restaurant with glaring
    florescent lights clean and hideous and we vow
    never to return again.

March 21, Wednesday

                    Spring Equinox
        when everyone flocks
            to Chichen Itza to see the royal snake
    descend the huge pyramid.

Dreams have me visiting
with Nancy, and Gin John who is entertaining
Magda. And two gay ladies who run a bookstore
in their home but seem to have dropped the
poetry section. Trying to find a place to
put a small bundle of gardening tools. Leave
them in Margo Doss's Bolinas basement, where
Sandy has left his bed unmade. Sister
Margaret around there. Simone has some sort
of accident with a Mexican truck, drawing
lots of attention to herself and gets Bill
Kornblat, the Bolinas painter, to help her
translate. I must return to my car to pick
up Gin John—

And get a wonderful ride on
the back of a shining black horse behind a
handsome Mexican whom I hold on to. The
horse moves so easily. Galloping, the motion
is superb, I shift my weight slightly.

We pass emerald green fields, interspersed
with dry yellow grass fields that are to be
burned. An adjacent dry grass field might
catch fire, and the rotund mustachioed
Mexican foreman rushes over to see it doesn't
spread. Near the Olema Cemetary. We are on
the way from Pt. Reyes to Bolinas.

Marcello, our hotel keeper, says there
are white long-haired monkeys here in the
wild jungles of the Yucatan, like Orangutans,
called Saraguato.

Diana: 'I've fucked up again.'
Cleaning a spot on her wall it gets bigger
and bigger. 'They'll have to repaint the
entire room.'

March 24, Saturday

Swimming at Progreso Beach, the day is
hot. Cool coconuts. Top is thwacked off,
straw inserted, taken from cooler at stand
run by three little boys today.
Who never go to school?

Diana gets letter
from Shao, he can't afford to leave. Ed. P.
having big party March 18 at 'Joanne's'.
Bill McNeill's funeral to be at RCA
first week April.

'I don't want to go back.
I want to go on.'

What *really* to pay attention to.

What drivel in the 8:30
pent up evening Donald reading the spy story
holds him hard as life now the rain has
stopped and there isn't much else to do.
Charles Olson line back to *Mayan Letters*,
Allen Ginsberg on the Adivino,
Bill McNeill's Red Tori,

Vermillion the gateless gate.

We lie on the Beach a long time
and swim

March 25, Sunday

They're parked in a big
semi rig across the street, no load on
the back   Sunday night courtship
a hand pats the back of her brown
white bloused body, later her head
of black hair lies on the open window
ledge of the truck door; immaculate white

clad Sailors with night sticks walk by in
night patrol stroll
across the street from this table which peers
now over the balcony . . .

                    Little Yucatan parrot
          on the Unicorn today a 32 foot
          sailboat at Puerto Abrego's dredged out
            harbor at Yucalpeten, the northern tip
      of this peninsula. Bonnie and Steve
getting their boat worked on,
                          to sail on with their bright green
          bird friend. They lost another one at
Sea, nowhere to rest when it flies
  off and they find its body 20 minutes later
floating on the waves

            —big water, small bird . . .

March 26, Monday

          See Bill McNeill

      talking to Dr. John Doss last night in my
      dreams, he is heavy, almost fat, but his eyes
      are dark colored, like someone with hepatitis.
      In good spirits he is showing a canvas
      painted in two parts
                          of a Moon light path
      across the waters in silver and gold,
      from one existence into another.

          He is very proud of this painting.

Adolescent futzed
   the delightful fish
      Don brings
to someone in shrunken
white pants, El Salvador's
      election newspaper
         Monday morning
      coffee gringo's search
         for meaning of Spanish
   in between septic smells
      and Yankee California dope
         grown dollars
      that allow the privileged
   school of Mayan Yucatan
      English textbook Wa Wa
      brain.

A longer desire for Spanish still, to take me
down to the politics heart and tongue of
books I still pass up.

Pop! Pop in the 9 o'clock hotel door small
Alligator Leg from young boy this morning
looking to open beer bottle on inside
Volkswagon door at beach front road for
his father.

So Cool Donald quickly offers his
Swiss Army knife opener. The boy looks up
annoyed. Amazed! Thanks a lot as he flips off
the top and Pop on the wall says Otra Mas
and passes it on to us as we walk the round
cold Corona back to Room #2.

March 28, Wednesday

The heat seems almost fatal
as Panama hat and Margo Doss's tablecloth
are walked thru the noon sun where Diana
meets us at Casa Bowen table with Tequilla.
Farewells are said amid Caribe's outside
patio dinner and two senseless plastic bags
purchased for packing non-existent objects.
A little wooden violin.

March 29, Thursday

We depart via taxi,
plane up and down to Mexico City, Puerto
Vallarta, Zihuatanejo, San Francisco. Zip
thru customs and Immigration and wait
for Edward who takes us straight to Bolinas
and house as we left it.

Dream this morning has my
Mother and I having dinner. My Mother asks,
How is your little daughter, did she get
better?
         No, she died. Ah! Tears fall.

         Bill Brown is having fun,
driving around . . .

MATTER

or giving

In memory of Jack Boyce

I'm looking for a house to live in. Just a 1 bedroom house. We're expecting a baby 4 months from now, and we had to leave the place we were. It's a low muggy day. I'm not sure where anything is here. I watched the fishermen cut a marlin. A man with a nice face in shorts was splitting sections of bamboo and in back of him, the frame of a house made of branches & rope.

I climbed up in the hills back of the roads. A japanese family was up there walking along the rocks. Dusty chicken raisers & backward mechanics settled up here with the leaves & branch peelings & the rock, concrete, junked things. Outside of the depots, all is water, and heat, and dust, ants & mosquitoes. No salt. No sugar. Maybe some homemade vinegar, some dried tobacco. No kerosene. No yeast.

My neck & arms burn. I take a seat on lava rock. It's not that this is where I'd want to stay. There is no pleasure but the physical one of being here. I wipe the sweat down. Otherwise this is to report no luck. This is to report I know nobody. It's okay.

We came here on the "Stranger in Paradise."

These were Americans searching ease in the orient,

never leaving Paradise, their ideological capital,

to look at the earth.

It was dark, it was black
when I took the ferry back
& the land lay around me pine trees
& I had a bundle under my coat
& it was a new born baby

The baby did wake
we pissed in the salt
& the baby cried full mighty
so we moved over by the workingmen
tipped my hat & sat with them

And I heard this—

why do you want direction, are you seasick,
does what needn't be love you? why?
when? . . friend to stars

THE STRANGER

Sailor,
Stranger in town, where have you been—
what have you seen?

I leaped the cowgate & took to sea. My song woke the engine, under the bunker charge. That boat is gone. My friends were from other countries. I washed ashore. My song heard me, & sent me flood & desert. I looked at buildings from an old barge, people flowing down streets, meeting in cafes & train stations & theaters, people shutting doors & parting. I would go on.

I stood rude & hungry. I drank in plain bright shady stands by the road, with townspeople. My boss sent for me & I went, looking in the doorways & alleys. I went out for a long time. Different companions, different wages.

I came thru a valley, & the frost of the highlands. The ships were like music. I raised hand goodbye to roof & bridge & garden & my song was still not thru. Other lands, a year of northern fish. A low & ashen land, the people & trees were things all cinders & debris. I walked blond & floppy in a loose blue shirt to the south, rolling meadows, & red, oaten, sweltering families. Inconclusive labors. One time there was coral, piles of bananas on deck. Then poverty, & a dresser with chipped green paint. Wildness, or people like flies, & the uncertainty, the voices, the poorness down the halls, the battlefields of the world.

My song hurt me. I grew tired & bare. I went loco after the factory towns.

My lips got numb. I watched the moon in the river. I followed deer, I lived with squirrels, & my song strengthened me. I held people's babies while they ate. I was an idiot. I sat & watched the blinding red & yellow of women weaving. I caught a horse from the fire & spoke with it. I no longer cared if I would get there. My clothes were splayed. I put arms & legs to use, & took to the field with blanket & hat, deep in the clouds, wherever it might be best to change.

> Oh Stranger are you coming tonight?
> Are you done with your laughing & crying?
> For you I was saving whiskey & tongue
> Oh stranger—man husband father King—
> what brought you home?

*   *   *

My wife is washing dishes in the back of the restaurant, I can see her over one of the counters in the kitchen. She is feeling sick tonight (pregnant). I'm sitting out at a table with a beer she slipped me. Another waitress, the Sheriff's wife, is talking to a carpenter named Burr. I think about the stuff in the wiring and plumbing behind the wall, out to the poles on the street. Somewhere a river is dammed. I'm flipping through a couple of drugstore paperbacks. One is a pamphlet called *The Astral World*, by Theron Q. Dumont, first printed in 1912. The other's a french reporter's book on the old Manhattan Project: *The Untold Story of the Making of the Atomic Bomb*. Theron Q. Dumont is interested in spiritualism & self-improvement—in fact, on the back page are ads for other works such as *Guide to Public Speak-*

ing for Businessmen. "If you want to make the most of yourself, enter at will into the spiritual world, open the highway to bigger things, etc., etc." "A Chicago paper in a recent editorial said: 'There are men in this country in abundance, but good men, while in great demand, are as scarce as the clams in chowder at a church supper.'"

A fifty year dislocation of public knowledge into which the State Department flew the refugee scientists. By 1946 physicists could no longer be supported by non-governmental sources. And there's a leap—from Heisenberg's initial atomic physics seminar in Leipzig attended by a single student, to, twenty years later, the 'Manhattan Project' hiring 150,000 americans for its secret assignment.

We've seen that most of it is transitional because need manifests as the cry for a more complete energy transaction. One can't foresee a growing population with fossil fuels as the energy means—it is up to industry or mortality, not the designs of the past. A complete energy conversion, & complete recycling conversion without functional misappropriations, is the possible goal. But now 75% of the electronics industry is for war. It is designed and manufactured to kill. Bluntly.

Is that understood? There is a strain in the sky. The wind hums slightly now, coming on through town. Next to us is a building site with a parked caterpillar crane. There is a house next to that which is not yet dozed, but the septic tank is bust and detergent is all over the yard. From the porch the town sounds bitten off in the wind. Then way down the flats, there are cinders grinding at the edge of the sea and an old car sounds. On the porch the woman is rounding up kids and the man is stretching his bones. And now, when the sun's getting low and the lights of the awning of the movie house are on, and a truck with its hood is open, it's a red and white time with a large sky, a beer to spread the distance between work and supper. For a moment on the horizon there's almost a reversal, as the sun seems to move upward and there are round shadows under all the faces. Good and evil are forgotten and people are back outside. At last we want to live here. We went to the liquor store by the laundromat, got some beer, and Andy put it in the bag.

⋆   ⋆   ⋆

As the later term of vector, we're here—and every
thing's to be associated with someone being here . . .

20,000 years ago — last advance of the ice

1500 B.C. — Hittites smelt iron ore in Asia Minor

c. 500 B.C. —   enter with Anaximander.
               "He did not ascribe the origin of things to any
            alteration in matter. Into that from which things
            take their rise they pass away once more, for they
            make reparation and satisfaction to one another for
            their injustice according to the disposition of time."
         All injustice, even a hillside dug for shelter, is pro-
            posed as, in this instant, effectually and intrinsically
         given justice. So things have valence, and thus social
      organization, in what might otherwise be a society of strangers.
   The "ruler" is what it's like, and it is like

share (moira)

Hopi exchanges of equivalent values

or Tlingit redistribution

the "courtesy" of nature (Galileo)

the *eligibility* (kalaba) of the heart — Ibn Arabi

(Plato) The life of 'justice' in the 'soul'

or *information* in Norbert Wiener's sense
(exchange with the outside

Methexis (participation—thus valence, & retribution

or "what you give to the poor is what
you take at the moment of your death"
Ignatius & Jesuits)

Ruling & tropism   Reckoning & computare

or *karma-vipaka* (in oneself that moves one

out of oneself as retribution—
that makes one *move* to *give*, in
whatever case

* * *

such conduct is not to gain advantage, even in spiritual
material, but to establish a right to the accruing unfolding
expanse of giving, *originally* of the stimulus or the earth.

What is owed the benefit of the doubt gets it, and the 'personality'
or 'gnosticism' is only one need of assertion. The personal momentum
can't be lost, but given, shared, exchanged by transformation.
Many of the artifacts recovered by archaeology must have been gifts
testifying to and depicting this process, past ruin of all other
habitation.

    "How does one safeguard this place?"
    "Thru men."
    "By what are men gathered together?"
    "By goods."

★   ★   ★

"How shall the great-hearted Achaeans give you a prize?
We are not aware of any large common store lying available anywhere.
What things we took from cities when we sacked them have been distributed.
It is not proper that the people should reverse this and collect them back
and amass them again."

(*Iliad*, Book I)

Self discipline and town discipline, parts of the Ionian physics,
were gone in Alexandria by the 3rd Century B.C. Science had begun
to serve war. Nature had descended into a cosmos, as Plutarch

later said. And towns were herded by soldiers and priests.
Anaximander's sense of the returns *outside* of perception is
missing, two or three hundred years later, in Aristotle.

★   ★   ★

I don't want to locate any thing in any time as a fait accompli, but to
suggest that the earth is self-judging in a jussive-potestative vision akin to
recent tensor calculus of continuous change and uncertainty.

The 'science' of the last millennia B.C. seems inseparable from experi-
ences of human rule & self-rule registered with *clarity*.

"Justice", in Anaximander's fragment, is as much its Indo-European
'root' *jeudh* (*to set in motion*), & that root's various sense-developments, than
the 'philosophical' or 'administrative' connotations it has come to acquire
since roman gubernaculum went for sale. Research here needs to be done
on underlying terms for energy, like the Hittite participle *para handanza*
("guided in the order of justice"), or its equivalents (?), Akkadian *misaru*,
Sumerian *nig.si.sa.*, etc.

Early terms for the organization of nature, fine & vulgar.

Where Anax says 'justice', physics would perhaps say *chance*, in the sense
of what befalls, or can be discriminated so to speak *in descent*.

★   ★   ★

Something has gone wrong, as if there were a limit to its
motion. The old day is dissipating. It is time for something
stunted, without hunger. It hurts, until there is no worth,
but silence and heat.
Is it loneliness, of this land?

2 lines

4 lines

2 lines
2 lines
TV
reception

wires in
the
air

```
I  DO NOT WANT TO BE A COMPUTER PROGRAMMER
DO I  NOT WANT TO BE A COMPUTER PROGRAMMER
I  DO NOT WANT TO BE A COMPUTER PROGRAMMER
I  DO NOT WANT TO BE A COMPUTER PROGRAMMER
I  DO NOT WANT TO BE A COMPUTER PROGRAMMER
I  DO NOT WANT TO BE A COMPUTER PROGRAMMER
I  DO NOT WANT TO BE A COMPUTER PROGRAMMER
I  DO NOT WANT TO BE A COMPUTER PROGRAMMER
I  DO NOT WANT TO BE A COMPUTER PROGRAMMER
I  DO NOT WANT TO BE A COMPUTER PROGRAMMER
I  DO NOT WANT TO BE A COMPUTER PROGRAMMER
I  DO NOT WANT TO BE A COMPUTER PROGRAMMER
I  DO NOT WANT TO BE A COMPUTER PROGRAMMER
I  DO NOT WANT TO BE A COMPUTER PROGRAMMER
I  DO NOT WANT TO BE A COMPUTER PROGRAMMER
I  DO NOT WANT TO BE A COMPUTER PROGRAMMER
I  DO NOT WANT TO BE A COMPUTER PROGRAMMER
I  DO NOT WANT TO BE A COMPUTER PROGRAMMER
I  DO NOT WANT TO BE A COMPUTER PROGRAMMER
I  DO NOT WANT TO BE A COMPUTER PROGRAMMER
I  DO NOT WANT TO BE A COMPUTER PROGRAMMER
I  DO NOT WANT TO BE A COMPUTER PROGRAMMER
I  DO NOT WANT TO BE A COMPUTER PROGRAMMER
I  DO NOT WANT TO BE A COMPUTER PROGRAMMER
I  DO NOT WANT TO BE A COMPUTER PROGRAMMER
I  DO NOT WANT TO BE A COMPUTER PROGRAMMER
```

yr fingers in
my hair
mama I don't
care

The relationship of living is that of a poor man to the earth, penetrating to uncover the source of giving.

The human animals I call poor in the sense of poor in spirit, satisfied by sustenance—indigenous. Science & industry disallow them & organize them in a false nature. The old way of life is made to seem illegal—a path to poverty & contempt, or the result of evildoing. But because broken being may mean less penetration one must choose between the one cent of his mind, or the million dollar world without it. Industrial conversion breeds a creation that is tasteless, spiritless, that can only be maintained by a chemical mechanical environment. It's energy crises remind of let them eat cake. Each technological aid is a symbol of the ultimate failure of man on earth. Maximum production, plus devices to straighten it out ecologically, all some factitious way to keep the mind out of the rain for a couple of generations. It is only mental, it doesn't enter the person's spirit. Behind the scenes the real issues become theories of disposal and population control. Poets have been pointing this out from the start. Hazard Adams in an exposition of Blake's visions puts it bluntly—"the substance of materialism is the creation of human agony from nature." That's to say, if the material world alone is restored, that world's very success becomes a curse. In this sense a placental Nature is the misery of others, in formation. This nature in turn backs up an eye which merely observes "sights". Baudelaire drew a similar deduction: "Progress (in so far as it exists) sharpens suffering in proportion as it refines sensual pleasure, and if the skins of peoples get even more delicate, they are evidently pursuing nothing but an *Italiam fugientem*, a conquest lost again . . ."

No world to conquer exists in itself. In this case what has not been perceived is responsibility for the earth. Without that responsibility, a wide range of technological aids placed over it may have been worse than nothing. The phenomenological characteristics of matter aren't so much what it *looks* like, but where we are headed.

The reentry is infinitely open

I'd consider research or applied science to be the use of money to save human energy, i.e. money is necessary for getting people to work in sequence on one effort, secure materials, operate complex equipment, etc. But as Blake says "For every Pleasure Money is Useless"—so, from the point of view of *saving* human energy, the overall cost/benefit ratio is a curse necessary only while getting the job done.

Science has laid the crash program permanently on the people. Participation is not voluntary, & there's no sign that the job will ever get done. It is a maintenance operation with no organization particularly concerned with where daily life is coming from. Meanwhile people are required permanently to pay for things that have already been paid for—so live a drain off of energy implied to be temporary. Who paid for N.Y.C., Menlo Park, likewise Moscow, etc.... This is *people*, who are taken for a ride day after day.

The earth is already a life-support system, but the gleam in people's eyes changes to what is never enough. The standard of living must be maintained or improved—therefore automate, make *everyone* richer. When farmers started producing 'surplus' the direction of production should have changed, but the people were not up to it, they were somehow exhausted. If the paycheck is neither needed nor given, but just sits there like oh rose thou art sick & fallout shelters—What is available is not beautiful, & the trees, which flower by force, set no sustaining fruit—and on the outskirts of Miami, & Palm Beach . . .

I see a broken limb & the buds which must still flower . . .

Ignore the service
  no matter whether
    sacred or profane—

& see the human cry
built on, to cut us
  offf from pain

(*Machines*)

I pray, I pray, I pray, I pray
even if I only got a bone to gnaw

& there's nothing but stars when I'm alone
that I have the dignity

in this false home
cause main street, that's all a loan

and blood, that's all a loan
and grace

is as
low as

the earth.
Teach us

Saint Francis
how to give

—thru human
desire. Not

for you. Not for
my love, but for

an unfamiliar
stranger. It's

new.

The house I am working at is simple and white. Building a fence. The line for the fence has changed 6 times. A car goes by. Then a horse. I don't know what I'm going to do next. My partner's fixing the wiring inside the house. A car passes the other way. There's a kid watching me work with the post hole digger. Smoke drifts from the house and into the air. I'm staring at a broken lawn-mower. I take my shirt off. Throw it on a pile of splintered boards and wire and chunks of concrete. The truck stands hot, shining in the afternoon. The grasses sway. What an ugly house. A wall and 4 garbage cans. Then I think of people talking about mind over matter. Remember they are sitting under a roof in cheap enough clothes, presumably electricity is coursing thru the walls. What is meant is energy, ecstasy. Everybody is a head these days (California). Someone wants me to agree that the body is a projection, that there is entry into some magnetic inner world that might influence the world. A kind of dashboard lit up by mental power. We are in a sort of free medical clinic that at times seems like a place to hang out. There are pamphlets about V.D., magazines, a copy of the I Ching. The people are important in a dreamy sort of way. Mind over matter, a kind of mental power with one's eyes closed and in silence.

Still I was thinking, is it an illusion that cans of chopped meat sit filling shelves in grocery stores. Did I project the life of cattle ranging from the Argentines thru Paraguay, to the Brazilian coast then southern Chicago and out in truck trailers? I can't understand a mind projecting end products as is. It's much too fortuitous. Perception is particular in its hungers. It's the fans, borrowers and persuaders who make it *other* worldly. Somehow akin to turn-of-the-century puritans. I was thinking of Christian Science and the effort of that time to put the mind over the top. Mrs. Eddy connects matter with *error*—or what the mortal mind believes it senses. That would be right in some way for the incredible sights of the late nineteenth century. That unanswered question, can we relieve pain (death) without medicine? By will? Can we leave the world? A kind of incomplete inspirational wind, side by side with pragmatism, that went where? I suppose it comes from that old question, does death end all? So Mary B. Eddy proposes that matter can take no cognizance of itself, and I can see the street ripped up with board fences and manholes, masons & carpenters standing by stripped buildings, radios playing from a hot dog stand. Lincoln Steffens returns from Russia: "I have seen the future and it works." A clerk & a salesman are arguing in front of a bar where old people watch T.V. and across the street the subway is letting a thousand people out.

I split, I was only there for my lunch hour anyway. It's hard to think of an 'american' mind in relation to the many other cares. That mind's really pathetic loathing of materialism, with simultaneously no relationship to act on such an ever multiplied scale. Think you're going to solve the future in a half hour? Ya! For all of it the trucks still weigh as much. We're here to absorb the opposite momentum. It'll eventually all return and now it feels as inexhaustible as the sky to a child. Back to work.

picked up again

Science is oriental if anything, it doesn't begin in europe
til the 16th century when it ceased to parallel philology.

Henry the Navigator's school in Portugal

Widman's *Commercial Arithmetic* Leizpig, 1489

Naval operations. Artillery etc. Indies

Patents 1624 England (privatization of public knowledge)

300 orchard trees were shipped to Massachusetts Bay 1630.
South Carolina got rice from Canton a little after 1677.

Leibniz — *De Analisi Situ* (origins of vector)

1750 "Physiocracy": "only land contributes anything in excess of
    production costs; wealth has no value beyond the possibility of
    exchange."

Arkwright mills 1768 Nottingham England

1776— American decolonization coincides with discovery of hydrogen.
    That superseded the old element matter.
    Vide Gaston Bachelard.

Jefferson's Garden Book 1776–1824 (His remark, in a democracy there shd be a revolution every 20 years, from this point becomes less constitutional & more a question of energy conversion ratios)

photosynthesis— 1796

"continuous & leisurely Experiment"

Engineering, the last 150 years

Industrialization— last 3 generations

Electron— last 75 years. At which point machines
            are only partly 'mechanical'. 'Mechanical'
            matter goes to its gaseous upper limits,
            something Henry Adams notices. After that, each
            machine draws the line between 'mechanic' &
            'electric' differently (The line is in the form of
            a medium). Matter is stored energy charge.

organs as link of 'mind' & 'matter' —e.g. Sir Charles Bell on movements of
            eye-muscle etc. (going back at least to 1550, Dr. Jean Fernel)

The RR :: was private property (1869– transcontinental U.S.)

        1835 Frederic Bastiat: "value is the cost of replacement depreciated."

            Joint stock companies — 1860's

Jeremy Bentham, legislative psychology for the colonies

Multinational Corps start around 1900   The Pacific

1897–1902— joining of railroads & multi-plant entities (example: U.S. Steel)

"8 hours shall be
damned a day's work" (1916)

Air is Power

1924–29 — mergers of manufacturing, pub. utilities &
merchandising (ex: G.E., I.B.M., Westinghouse)

Invariantheorie (rather than relativity theory)

Broadcasting: imaginary 'real' life of everything:
the time, the weather, will John marry Marsha, etc.

1926— 1st TV network

1928— renunciation of idea that a model is necessary
(Quantum Mechanics)

Electromagnetic forces: gamma rays

Isotopes (2 or more possessed by all known elements—
All elements on earth heavier than uranium
have already 'died')

Computer, unbalanced components & modules, able
to accept a million instructions per second

Bombs— a BILLION DOLLARS each

Plasma— most common form of matter in the universe
(Gravity is shown to be a local peculiarity)

1965–8 — conglomerates —ex: Textron, Litton, N. American
Rockwell, I.T.T., Shell

"automation" — permanent reeducation by dominant media

1st creation of an anti-element in 1965, England

& now the age of either making a star *on* earth or
a star *of* earth

One could throw in as a final date 7,000 A.D.—when Fred
Hoyle says the mass of humanity would exceed that of all planets, stars, &
galaxies visible with the Palomar telescope.

There is a primary drive, say, displaced.
The earth fractured prime. Oh did they
only want it to divide, in dense interactions
to trade it for something of greater
value? Niels Bohr, Edward Teller,
can those men know what *pain*
is? Can they feel pain at this life re-
turning, the question of whether it will
return, unless for them it can't
return. 35% of the earth's energy
consumed, the United States
dynamo cooking away like a
story that ends at the top
(the sewer pumped up to the penthouse), the top
of the sucker list, the bot-
tom of generation. There
are no heroics from the
point of the big toe (trapped
in a trainee or italian
stiletto shoe). *Pairidaez*
is not at the top
& the grand carnival drop from
tumescence.
It's all a livid tale in
the veins of the feet, & any
matter which must be raised
in order to rest.

By now we have started pruning. I checked out a pick leaning up against the shed by the water tank, stopped for a mouth of water & under the tank's spigot I noticed slugs crawling around the chunks of drain rock. The water tank is huge, a landmark. We're clearing coffee, cutting trees & small growths—more tiny snips & cuts than a man could do in his whole life, just on these few mountain acres. I hold a thick branch & chop at it, feeling the wet fiber against the machete, thru the twigs. Behind are stumps and the ground is littered with branches and big dark curled leaves. The back of my T shirt is wet. I see my wife's red face with a bandana around her hair, her faded bluejeans moving thru the brush. She is followed by a sick dog, over the dry brush piles. A family of fools in the wilderness, like everyone around here. Fifty acres over the horse raising people are warring with the cattle raising people, as if they'd turned independent of each other. Someone else knocks out a couple of acres of coffee to raise michihili. For sale signs go up on a road in complete disrepair. Then there's one cowboy who just sits around and carves hardwood weapons with a penknife. He's useless when he's sober, but with a hit of acid he starts whittling & rubbing & pretty soon faces start coming out of the wood, & he wets them with dribbles of spit. He's not planning to make $10,000 in the next two years, or whatever keeps the great things going. My neighbor comes home in the afternoon from his job. He says hello to his wife and new baby, then goes to the closet and gets out his shotgun—an extra long model made for gun clubs. He gets about 10 vitamins & a beer, then goes out back in the morning glories & shoots his gun off into the trees.

So are we too, cutting & slicing away, til my hand is locked in the shape of a saw handle. We took it away from the morning fields, the beautiful moment of simple protection, fields & mountains naturally changing, choked with debris, was not enough. The original river of land is not enough.

Also my wife and I have been dismantling an old building. A coffee shack, extended out with rock wall, beams & corrugated tin. The flooring is very spacious, tongue-and-groove, hardwood boards. Instead of walls there is hanging canvas blowing back & forth. There's the chute for the dried coffee to be loaded down, & a washing trough. The whole roof slides off, rolls back for sun or rain. But that was under the plantation system, when most of these buildings back in the woods went up. Labor was 10 cents an hour, contract labor for 3 years. Forty years ago. A few years back goats were penned underneath. In the high weeds around it are dry rusty nails, brake fluid cans, junk like that. The mountain burns up the four wheel drives pretty regularly. The big trees hum with flies, the green leaves look gray and far away—down to the heat reflecting highway. A few great trees have been given so much attention that they have human conscious standing. A person passing thru the towering groves could talk to them. Or a dog. Does that seem funny? All we can give, at least, is a place to live. Wherever a person is cared for, guided helplessly as a whole, amazed—

The building is half finished. Everything looks off level to me, my eyes strain. The unequal lay, the worn lines of speed sawing at an angle, at the ends, over space. Well.

I'm checking over my hands. The skin below the nails is nicked & bleeding, there's sawdust in my socks, little blue ridges of dirt in my nails. I had a splinter in my finger, but since then my hands have been smashed & burned & I don't hardly notice. I poke at it like it was a strange thing, & what a strange thing it is, a finger. All the headlines have disappeared. Consider a finger or toe. If pick & shovel ain't directly related to the Smithsonian, then it's your terms, or is there some mistake? Doesn't attention fail right *here*?

Erthe out of erthe is wonderly wrought;
Erthe hath of erthe a dignitee of nought;
Erthe upon erthe hath set al his thought
How that erthe upon erthe may be heigh brought.

Erthe upon erthe wolde be a king;
How erthe shal to erthe thinketh he no thing;
When erthe biddeth erthe his rents home bring,
Then shal erthe from erthe have pitous parting.

Erthe upon erthe winneth castels and towrs;
Then saith erthe unto erthe, "This is al ours."
When erthe upon erthe hath bigged up his bowrs,
Then shall erthe for erthe suffre sharp showrs.

Erthe gooth upon erthe as molde upon molde;
So gooth erthe upon erthe al glittering in golde,
Lik as erthe unto erthe never go sholde;
Yet shal erthe unto erthe rather than he wolde.

Why that erthe loveth erthe wonder me think,
Or why that erthe for erthe swete wil or swink:
When erthe upon erthe is brought within brink
Then shal erthe have of erthe a wonderfoul stink.

        Erthe took of erthe with wogh;
        Erthe other erthe to the erthe drogh;
        Erthe laid erthe in erthen throgh;
        Thanne hadde erthe of erthe erthe ynogh.

When the earth was fixed to a certain degree, it was given. Yet the present world could not be happening at the energies naturally available on earth. The paradox is that the relationship of life is that of a poor man to the earth. And the big shot says—Keep it protected, from agony—as it makes war.

The earth is the whole example to a poor guy. For example take water. The water on top of a mountain is pure but the water at the foot of the mountain has perhaps been spoiled in transit. So there is a cycle of water: it begins sweet, then acquires (mineral) salt, then becomes sour, then becomes bitter, and finally becomes pollution and poison, until it has been cleared by another cycle of the earth, with or without human aid. The water cycle also has meaning religiously, and in terms of the tastes of men, and as a metaphor for the stages of human life, and as a parable of relationships of creation in the heavens. The water is recognized as a grace, as one of the angels of humanity.

The big shots in towns have diverted this cycle to the point where few see it—the water may be sweet one day, salt the next, sour the next, bitter the next, and poison the next, but there's no control or awareness of it. The instincts of the Dante in each man are destroyed. The machines do it; taste and awareness are destroyed, until it doesn't matter.

But in the process machines are destroying the poor guy as well. The poor are killed in wars, colonized, relocated, conned by cash flow from the cities, given the illness and pollution that accompany the power age. The machines intended to be *preventive*, pain-relievers, protect and insulate only a state monopoly.

At this point I would be dogmatic. People *own* nothing; all people are poor. The owners are the gods, & people of earth who at this accrued date are no longer alive, so their "private" (inimicus) efforts have by now become "public" thoroughfares for poor people. I am not talking about the false poverty created by money, I am talking about all contemporary man. Since the

18th century all buildings streets furnishings machines & vehicles have been the work of essentially unknown constructors, who themselves owned only a partial feeling (demand) of what subsequent folk will always take over in a slow perishable cycle. This is the permanent revolution in the mansions of the dead constructors, either it's Greece or Peru or Cambodia or Morocco. The owners are a pretext in most ecologies. They are absentee, and exist for the most part in a resentful democratic imagination, probably because heredity has changed so swiftly.

Don't misunderstand me, businessmen perpetuate the owners as cause. And those are the hands that hold the decision-making, sure. But there is no loyalty implied there. When a man denies that he is poor, he has left the example of the earth behind and must draw analogies from a consumption that is random disposal and technological control. Everything is then seen to be in need of "improvement" in some absolute way. The consumptive sector grows more & more alarmed at its ghettoes, industrial slums (what Reason calls "pollution") but which is a return back to the festering earth on the part of the takers who have converted it to filth or qualitatively "evil" (repugnant) aspects of earth. Arrogance finally sickens at the sight of the destruction of the earth by parasites who might have made it fruitful.

I've seen the strangers, I've seen the people in servitude running, hiding, dodging. One feels that reaction on the street, to the presence of all those not involved. Wow. Kids, old people, ill people, blacks, women, those who can't read or write, foreigners, anyone with a low or zero income, anyone "strange," people in the wrong place at the wrong time, depressed, in pain, strangers to strangers—Oh, no. Those are people who have not yet merged with opportunity to save energy. The modern state might have hired social workers to explain what's going on, but think of the confusions, there's just too many of them, too diverse, they don't register to vote, they keep moving and moving. . . .

Ah baloney. That's how many folks on the street are marked.

They'll never know what hit em.

Get used to walking around em.

There is a bitter natural power that will come to meet the protected city environments. It is a javanese or malayan condition of animal degeneration genetic breakdown disease, parasitism, moving wherever earth as a fact touches earth as a fiction of science. It can be seen pervasively in dreams. It is life returning despite the attempts to defy it. Artaud called it the plague. That the end is *physical agony*.

When science becomes "Russia or America could wipe us all out in a few hours," I know it won't end there. Brother, that's nothing. We'll move on to more far out things, I don't doubt it for a minute.

But do you realize what you're saying?

Look, my friend, once you've stopped watching the sky, & the dawn, & have stopped praising—I don't give a shit who you are, 'cause you ain't. It is each person's valent right to participate, to be surrounded by animals, to see the condition of 7 stars at midnite, to cry & vocalize. Assyria could have told us. But some people are still hiding in the mountains. They believe what comes thru them from inside. Animals come out. We

will all die. What is inside? A blind man.
A monkey dressed like the president. Empty

houses. A pregnant woman. A corpse.
Benigno stands with a sword. A dog walks

round the mutilated lion who devours the
slaves that made civilization possible.

Rain came down on the half-finished construction site, the long lengths of wood in dark piles. It was gray and bright in the rain and the muddy trenches were draining the water out. The slope brought water down from a field above, & a fence.

There were 2 women in the house with their babies. One woman's milk had dried up, on a visiting trip. Things were tense, there wasn't much to do except go to the movies. The baby howled a lot while the milk dried up. Now she is peeking out the top of a baby pack, aloof. Burbling in the mild rain sounding world, very much in her own life for the moment. The other, slightly younger baby, stares with indifference—an intent, unreacting face. Neither baby could be forced into any conception, they have already taken place. And hang there, as an inorganic relation. No love or hate yet.

The women were discussing pregnancy & children, material to make shirts, family memories, other endless things. I saw Marlon Brando refuse the Academy Award on TV, my dad got angry but my mom thought it was great. I feel happier than yesterday. When there's nothing to do it's easy to feel low energy. Then there's the rain, and the staying inside a lot. The talk of people downtown, of trucks & dogs, work, food, families, interests me no more than who is right & who is wrong. The wild turkey someone got, the jeep broken, the flea infested puppies, the new class for midwives, all fades in the clearness of the afternoon. The windows are open, and around the house the rock and weeds are flattened by the mud, solidified, a more single dark thing.

The babies are nodding, full.

Would you like some more coffee?

The women are finally at ease, with hands resting on their bellies, laughing low. To think that it all came out of their bodies. Crazy! It's so matter of fact on the outside, so smooth. It's amazing how it holds together in there. Uh-huh.

Question: How has welfare & food stamps changed things since 1970?

Reply: Created a class of poor people who implicitly want to be rich but are unfamiliar with all former ways of doing so.

> Hippies etc. automatically raise the price of lousy land, lousy houses, lousy food—without doing anything with it.

I say: look who you think is
    hungry

They act like nobody wants anything but them.
They give a man flowers, that won't
make him strong, that don't fill needs.

> Then WHO makes the food
> on the table?

The least one can ask of a country devoted to consumption is that it close its mouth once in a while. I mean the U.S. has made its production invisible while boosting its *product* all over the place. At any rate since the forties. We know that homo sapiens is a rip off, and the 'dominant' of cultivation always fucks right *across* a circlical ecosystem in its attempt to keep the human scene going 24 hours a day, across even the life of its sun.

I suggest that part of science is akin to the mystery of the responsibility for fire. And that's not primitive, it's just been perverted by National Security, 19th century politics, and continuing. In lectures written in 1925 Prof. Whitehead pointed out 2 ills resulting from the first hundred years of the new power age: (1) ignoration of the true relation of each organism to its environment, & (2) the habit of ignoring the intrinsic worth of the environment in consideration of final ends. I can't imagine anyone quibbling with that or considering it primitive. All intellectual institutions (even the most traditionally serene) are polemic, and that's why Wm. Blake was such a dog face in connexion with the science & law of his time. Its front face is deism & parlor chemistry, its rear visage is sweat shops & the colonization of people by the state. Blake would say that what Newton leaves out so uglifies & demeans the world that it is a validity to beware of building on ("Sand", like). The most powerful values of divided man are the very ones which have lost most, & incarnated a spectrum to wail the loss, & wander ghostly, outside. The 19th century botched these responsibilities.

Something else comes from the upper Paleolithic and can perhaps be found to exist now. I take the example of rites of the Arunta people in central Australia. These ceremonies apparently defined how long a period of taking could last before it had to be given back. It's hard to tell. Intichiuma practices are complicated, and I'm not sure what they meant to a hunting & gathering people. To me they look like attempts to redeem both scarcity and abundance. The principle of Intichiuma is to affirm increase, by foregoing a temporarily destructive occasion of activity (like breaking the branch ends as the fruit is picked, or inbreeding, or genocide of a species—or anything pursued destructively too long). Periods of too great constructive activity (viz-the tower of Babel) are likewise sounded against all creatures created & destroyed in the process. These creatures are distributed as totems, and they are multiple matters corresponding to the many simultaneous materialisms of the environment. The system of multiplication & conservation is then allied to reciprocal gifts, as in marriage, and take the characteristic economic of one who cares. "They believed that the food-producing totem needed their help in procreation as they must ask his own for destruction" (G.R. Levy). This is life in the organization of nature, insofar as one lives with it the way one lives with one's love. But since *will* only applies to ends in one's power, the address to nature is within the movements of one's body.

You must think about this before pushing too many buttons. Someone might say, are you suggesting a return to totemic restriction or fellowship rather than science? No, no, no. I'm saying that the stranger's destination is gratitude. That people have been shrunken until there is rarely a grateful feeling. Culture without the seed is pointless, no matter how much cultivation is involved. The electricity goes on for no real reason, the same will be true of atomic energy. But somewhere, someone, pays for it. This is the modern distance: the ablation of presence. I am concerned because science isn't working on earth, and where it dominates people want to de-create the world. That's why the use of matter as an explanatory principle in physics seems a suspect sense. That's all. There's a confusion between the atom as a theoretical construct, an energy source, and a weapon—let alone how any child of the future is related to these divided facts. Related by economic propaganda and national defense for the most part. Why is the cure of human condition such a total occupational millstone? Why is it a negative relationship to the earth? Why has quantity supplanted personal interrelationships? Why is so much energy spent trying to escape from place?

These seem to me the relevant questions in human science, not how to further use people, or prevent certain human functions. The Intichiuma practice could reemerge as fasting publicly from what is overused, and feasting publicly from is underused, with no strings attached to any other preconception. But there is far more to be said. George Bataille suggests that War is an Intichiuma ceremony that originated ten or fifteen thousand years ago due to the identification of man and animals. A somber suggestion. Perhaps there is more to these rites, & their interplay of emergency and surplus, than has yet been admitted. Perhaps there is actually a larger context for Intichiuma: the killing of man by himself.

quotes from the literature

"Space is boundless by re-entrant form, not by great extension."
(Sir Arthur Eddington)

"No vegetable grows in vain."
(Joseph Priestley)

"The stages in this gradual course of deterioration of the surface of the earth & its atmosphere at the hand of man may be used inversely as an objective measure of cultural advance in human history."
(Carleton Coon)

"The greatest identity potential in the world today is that of *technical skill.*"
(Erik Erikson, 1966)

"Men do not disbelieve their Christ; but they sell him." (or—*exchange* him?)
(John Ruskin)

"Please be so kind as to thank the Minister, and inform him that I do not feel the slightest need of being decorated, but that I am in the greatest need of a laboratory."
(Pierre Curie)

"What have you gentlemen done with my child? You have debased this child, you have sent him out in the streets in rags of ragtime, tatters of jive and boogie-woogie, to collect money from all and sundry."
(Lee deForest, to executives of the radio industry)

"Commerce is return of the loan, a loan in which there is the understanding: give me more than I give you. For the merchant, even honesty is a financial speculation. Commerce is satanic, because it is the basest & vilest form of egoism."

(Charles Baudelaire)

"Once a government gets hold of something it never lets go."

(Leo Szilard)

"You will not understand what is necessary in the way of scientific control unless you are the first subject in your experiment."

(J. B. S. Haldane)

"I do not intend to publish any future work of mine which may do damage in the hands of irresponsible militarists."

(Norbert Wiener, 1950)

"No one shall be subject without his free consent to scientific experimentation."

(United Nations Bill of Human Rights)

"The U.S. military establishment is the largest organization in the world."

(Adam Yarmolinsky)

"We're hell on wheels."

(General George Patton)

Now the moment honors you Tartars
& things approach from a far distance
fatigued with the lowness the earth shows them
more sheep for your vertical nations.
"The Poor arrived in Fords, whose faces
they resembled." R-Rarf! R-Rarf!
It's Alexander of Macedon! The hills
& points of light come in like sheep. And
what else is there to possess, gray

Viking? Spare me a moment.
I know you're a turn in the Stranger's
journey. Tell me of your taste
for Everything, tell me of your readiness
to take it *all*. You solved the earth

as an orbit of goodness, & that was
an agonizing lie. So take
your time and shove it. And take
back your sun on the way out.
I suspect you planned to anyway,
you fucking homeless monads—

Finally you only get what you give
empty heart, a star broken, a
science of sand, your nature.

GANDHI

I was taking a piss one morning when I noticed a black furry thing under one of the banana trees. It was a strange dog & I nodded to him.

He hung around & during the day we took a look at him, a dirty hairy ghostly face with burrs stuck to it. He was old from his white hairs, painfully polite. Never barked.

So we threw out fish cans & he hung around the latrine, licking them. Or he would be asleep. We never really fed him. He followed us. Shit. We threw rocks at him. We loved him but he was an embarrassment. I can't see pets—not here. The other local dogs jumped all over him, but RAAA-A-AOAHHHH, threatening didn't affect him. He saw something else and followed.

He's a vague dog & when we'd go downtown he'd amble all over the highway—right in front of trucks and it's a busy highway with a lot of construction. It was a rip off, and one night near the baseball field a hot rod hit him at 50 miles an hour. It was dull and sickening to see him die. His spine was all bent & the rims of his eyes were bloody. As always he was completely silent. I carried him, part of the way it was hitchhiking, then up the mountain trail. The only food in the shack was, he couldn't eat it, a very fermented jar of fish. He couldn't eat.

He was alive the next day but would barely move his behind. He acquired a more shocked look. But had learned nothing.

Days after that when we walked into town we beat our brains to get him to stay, there in the trees & bushes on the mountain. But he was bowed down, never ingratiating, always apart.

I'd point to him—YOU—point—and yell like a fiend: *Leave us alone, god damn you.* But he had a murderous look, abstracted & patient. He was too nowhere to hit with the rocks anymore, I knew he would limp on in the highway, right of way, pretending to ignore. Til death. Never closed his eyes.

Back at the shack I tied him double to the bed and blocked all possible escape with chairs & boards. We'd leave, curse him, get all the way down the rubbly trail, almost a quarter mile to the road, always looking back— and god damn that mangy simple-minded fucker would be creeping and creeping after us like a lizard. How he did it I could never figure out. The hateful, shambling thing. What does he live for? Not food certainly. Is he asking me to kill him? No. Is he lost? No. He comes on and on, a dogged blind passivity, peace that passeth all god damn understanding. He recalls all creatures who want to do nothing. No winter wipes it out. This is the mountain's doing, not mine. The life supporting mountains.

OH

The time
the floor
the company
the sound
the up & down
the stutter
the death
the breath
the inertia
the commemoration
the air
the heat
the danger
the installations
the partitions
 the earth
  the sun
    the delight
     the momentum
      the creepy crawl
        the appreciative
          the fatigue
          the safety
            the trepidation
              the efficacy
               the roll
                 the tickle
                  the secretion

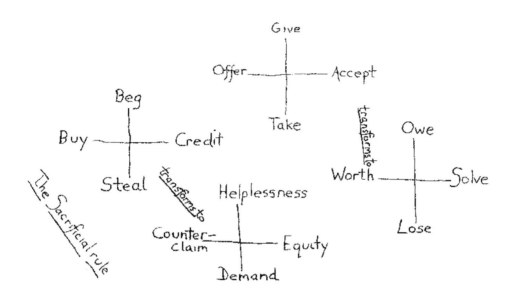

The earth gives
water. One takes
a drink of it.
One gives water

to another. One
gives, back. One
returns that.

★   ★   ★

Things don't take care of themselves. Things give people pleasure, and
the ruler derives from those things, with all the guilt of exchanges entailed.
A thirsty man must think of water, & water & its human need, become the
thing of a thing. Of each person lacking and each thing lacking, together.
The mood is imperative, rectification. There is no flattery possible here, &
probably no argument against it. In decay this is authority, the *right to con-
trol* those to whom one gives. But often at this point there's a limit reached
in feeling things for one's own use. One's use offends coherence. One is
stripped of the message. Suddenly the ruler has turned into a chump, the
room is full of only thugs & punks.

I'm trying to convey a sense of the price of activity. We could suppose
that Manu or Justinian, say, realized then that the ruler has to give up some
things in order for there to be one thing strong enough to bear the rest. In
the process there is sacrifice. A person has to give out something and take
something else, tho it looks like quits to conserved civilization. I think for
a physicist this was Leo Szilard's experience. What is sacrificed is an artifi-
cial matter; the body was begged, borrowed, and stolen from in an endless
chain of murders. At some point technology, intended to save life, took on

the role of redemption. There was a feeling of burden in many quarters, &
Emerson relayed the common sense that the world now owed more than
the world could pay, & ought to go into chancery and be sold for whatever
it might fetch.

Whether nuclear fission, or fusion, or magnetohydrodynamic produc-
tion, or solar cell conversion, become the means, is a question of what *would
be* (conditionally) worth human energy. There's no transfer to another con-
dition that doesn't require total transformation in the being that set out for
it. You want to talk about transformed condition? You will have to die and
give it all up anyway. There won't be these senses to do the thieving, instead
there'll be another message than what the senses have taken for themselves
all these years. Probably the decision provides the material as much as the
material. A man is mass, and there's no law about conserving that mass.
Chancery might convert it into other energies, along with all the buildings
and tools.

Nuclear fission converts about 0.1% of the mass of a heavy nucleus into
energy. With nuclear fusion, which leaves far behind the heat & pressure
of earth's ecology, the conversion is raised to perhaps 0.6%. The industrial
process involves 24 hour a day operation, breakdown, replacement, & con-
stant fluctuating costs. Initial phases are deeply mortgaged, involving all the
equity a transitional society can agree about. The power sources can only
be handled at a remove, & only with political clearance. The energy conver-
sion is never complete. There's the power of the seed, and the power of the
star, and the energy tensor of motion in both. I mean CHANGE/CHANGE.
The world left over in the environmental equation is then turned over, as
the commission, the charge to the heir.

Here redemption means restoration to life, & condition is that which is in force prior to action. "Will" is approximately the conditional form of verbs (the original past tense of "will" being "would"). It's as if we're affected by the generosity of the future, tho not able to live in it. Even with no overt "future" tense, there is valor or defeat within its proposal. Condition implies one was *there* in various states. It's a stipulation, and is different from the limitation that the Stranger feels (to his own ends). Only the creator can take advantage of condition. The Stranger is more a place in the ambiguity of will, from which all cautious impositions derive. It was Gandhi's contention that there's no such thing as a condition, meaning that we're only there by virtue of being *here*. And it is here before it is still here, etc. He did it, knocked out the whole Empire. In the same context I include Rule, because 'Things' grow, you might say they appreciate in certain epochs. There are periods of expanded power during which the stipulation enters and implicates other events. This subordinated man as future. So "condition" is one might say a state of the organism: it's the cure of the fact that we're the future people. One can take it on or give it back.

The process is more than given and giving, it's

(verbal auxiliary of

ought   own)

CONVERSION — a dedication of what WILL happen to one

owe

("owe" is a different
case of possession)

2. Sanskrit *yajamana*—
"he who expects the effect of his acts
to react on himself"—
literally,

sacrificer of his own

3)   a heritage of
self-possession
in turn owed
in retribution

Rule of this sort has been perverted by both power and puritanism, which mistakes the sacrifice. For example King Minos was supposed to have sacrificed *himself* at the end of 8 years. Instead he tried to substitute Athenian citizens. That conversion doesn't work. The materials aren't metaphoric, i.e. they're not *like* themselves. Man has the implicit value of what he's got or can get, that equity, to work with. Recall Alexander's observation: "Things make reparation and satisfaction to one another for their injustice according to the disposition of time." This far reaching remark combines worth, valence, & rule-in-organization. It is something far far earlier than morals. It's more like the thing that wants you to move. You are the locus of conversion.

Now suppose you don't know how to give. Suppose you don't know hospitality. Suppose you forgot what people like, what people need: Well, that's servitude, whatever the country or government. That's the people's way gone. Cause if nobody gives, people take.

There is only a little bit FOR SALE at any one time, a dish or two of food to eat daily. That everyone wants to live like a millionaire is a horseshit joke. Some people are terrified of owning even a cow or a duck—or would rather buy vegetables than gather them and possibly bring dirt in the door. Civilized pleasures? They want only the best, & that is murder of the human. Civilization is to say, *indigenous*. There's no sense in wanting more credit than the place gives. What, a billion rows of pea plants? Crowns of wild olive? Whatever you like.

If no one will go ahead with you; if your town won't come out for you; if the government isn't on your side; if public figures ignore you—this might all be just as well but the process breaks down from under-use. And the cities become artificial Mothers with shelters settled like science-fiction visitors—Matter feared again.

If you're hungry ask me for food. If you don't like my leather boot cooking, go ask someone else. It is horrible to see people breaking themselves & the animals & plants in half in privacy, because they don't feel able to say what's the matter & involve others as tribes did. It is up to you & me not to be a Stranger. No one else can do that. Do you think you can ever go back by yourself?

I thought of taking a truckload of guavas up to the cannery. The trees are so overgrown. Then the other day I was looking for the Greenwall Ranch Office way up on a hill, until I found out it was at the other side of the plantation, miles away.

So there's nothing much to do now but sit & enjoy the afternoon, a hint of rain, & the guava trees full & ripe, & in the west the removed beauty of the sun. I am shielded by a million stars for what is mine to give, my place to reenter, back on earth.

That is always there, and can't be taken from.

in an old wood shack up in the mountains
The Lion is cut open & people are marching out

Captain Cook, Hawaii, 1973

Appendix

E. Borregaard— *Analepsis* (unpublished)

H. Corbin— *Avicenna and the Visionary Recital*

P.A.M. Dirac— *Principles of Quantum Mechanics*

Sir A. S. Eddington— *Fundamental Theory*

R. B. Fuller— *Inventory of World Resources, Human Trends, & Needs*

Sir W. Hamilton— *The Elements of Quaternions*

Sir J.C. Maxwell— *Electricity & Magnetism*

Spencer and Gillen— *Native Tribes of Central Australia*

van t'Hoff— *Chemistry in Space*

Ezra Pound reminds me of a double warning when dealing with the historical usages of science. (1) That in the medieval era there was less 'material' science & more careful terminology ("the general exactitude may have been—probably was—higher"). and (2) modern science did not rise on this basis ("Science does not consist in inventing a number of more or less abstract entities corresponding to the number of things you wish to find out") but by an event in which something is effected specifically. With that caution, I'll lay down a residue of terms implicitly in the foregoing.

power— the rate of using energy
power— the ability to make profits by spending money
science— money (& slave skills)
Nature— a day
physics— enjoyment
history— groceries
Politics— the renting of money
The 'system'— a minority livelihood
multiplication— is distribution (Production—cf. "factory": interaction of
                small parts which might otherwise be dispossessed
Money— originally the one thing we chose not to destroy (Marcel Mauss);
                secondary meaning—restraints on revenue
exchange— directing of everything where it'll do that for which it was
                intended
Particle— "an object whose dimensions are negligible compared to the
                distance necessary to fix its position"
Field— the space proper to something
locus— a set of points satisfying *given* conditions
Valence— how much one can & will gain or lose; what is unneeded, what
                tends to have to give away
atom— a word not a 'thing' (& as consequence of literacy between men
                and women hasn't done much good since 1942 or 1919)
Conservation— commission controlling a natural site; cf. service
entropy— 'transformation-content' (*Verwandlungsinhalt*—Clausius.)
                Condition of a substance undergoing a reversible change
Now— adverb *and* conjunction
Engineering— cf. 'ingenious', to add to what's growing?
organization— what furthers its own interest
Conversion— cf. Sanskrit *vartate*—"it is turned, happens"—leading non-
                linearly back to Rule
redemption— dream

Giving— release of, or allowance at a loss (cf. "loose")
    Kinds of gifts (Physics & society—*Fasti*—inter vivos)
        1) Absolute
        2) to one for delivery to another
        3) to one as trustee

    example of a gift: Plutonium

"Sacrifice"— make an *offering*—to carry towards; present for consideration
        or as an act of devotion; to declare readiness; to try; or begin;
        to exert; to be available
        (Webster)
Evil?— limits to motion in growth of all organisms? Satan being gravity,
        or inadequate relation of matter to mass—a particular condition
        of earth; not as far as we know anywhere else
Dirt— shit (Old Norse) (2nd meaning is Earth, Ground—cf. matter in the
        Pistis Sophia hymns)
'surplus'— a quantity of production that will not go into consumption at a
        given price
Chaos— greek for "gas"

matter— given, to give

    "You paint the way you have to in order to give, that's life itself, and
    someone will look and say it is the product of knowing, but it has
    nothing to do with knowing, it has to do with giving."

    (Franz Kline)

ATTENTION

Watch-house
Point: to descry
anew: <u>attendeo</u>
& broadcast
the world (over the
<u>marshes</u> to the outer limits even where minutiae
hold & swim in the electro-magnetic
strain—and there are only seasons
to be there [at the outer places
       Ut gard Out-Yard when
those particular seasons (<u>days</u> actually hours
make it possible
(impossible: periods
not the same as
necessary
or contingent fate
  & grief love
   & knowledge

one house—
one father one mother one city

     Charles Olson

(Note: Imagining the following—<u>spoken</u> 'now' to Charles Olson—'says' that <u>narrative</u> <u>is</u> <u>what</u> <u>attention</u> <u>does</u>—that 'story' is what issues forth from the double occasion (to "descry" <u>and</u> "broadcast") "words in the mouth"—

"polis is / eyes" in this sense—that, <u>for Keats</u>, as public instrument—'looking' at 'the world' <u>given</u> by language process attention (to the "minutiae" therein revealed, seen-said / said-seen) called to particular 'waking' awareness & intensity in the "Ut gard" (which may well be the 'backyard') establishes, in & through the agency of such (<u>seeing</u>-) writing, the body politic—its names & laws & more primarily (?) its syntax, its narrative patterns—wherein we talk, as 'civilized beings'—

I looked up
and saw
I was faced
to the left

Okeanos,
the wobbling
ring

Attention, <u>viz</u>. invention & enactment of various 'syntaxes'—'paratactic' (only <u>vs</u>. conventional syntax?) says very little re actual ways & agencies opened & developed in Olson's project—is what "does" distinguish Olson's work <u>as</u> <u>writing</u>—that which looks sees that language 'follows' from joyful seeing—

'It doesn't exist in a vacuum'—i.e. is no static, or 'subjective', 'awareness'. "Attention" is a condition of this further showing—a sort of command (albeit 'exhausted') toward further <u>shape</u> for what <u>shall</u> occur & <u>may</u> 'prosper' as <u>narrative</u> is ('our part') allowed & empowered to <u>sound</u> the world.)

SEVEN NARRATIVES

I

What gets made (oats or), left, as evidence, from <u>narrate</u>—as noun, trace ('object') should still be able to 'motivate' reader back to 'activate' noun as a kind of dance floor/place for various activity (as, threshing)—record of a passage, verb initially, now much more complex, as composition enters in.

From <u>know</u> (cognate: 'cousins' at least), apparently (<u>related</u>)—how to 'grapple with experience' ('gnaw') by (having to?) think things in time 'somehow' gnosis/human, has to be ("has to be"?) + subsequently, how a people knows what's happened/happening—via present & available <u>can</u> do.

Or: sort of 'cultural DNA', with similar problems of origin—how to g<u>o</u>, how <u>it goes</u>.

Spuriously used as means to 'predict' the future.

What's 'time'—secret of narrative everybody tries to remember, because therein lies the shape of the world we see (only 'appears to be'?—no, <u>thus</u> truly appears, but only if bidden, given). Is/what was/can be.

But what if composition is an illusion, <u>vide</u> dusty field glasses, and nobody can tolerate being <u>told</u> anything about 'estimating' scale, range, power, accuracy of equipment because they shake their tits at this banal thingifying of the work-in-itself? The work-in-itself (anything pushed forward could be a 'narrative' sufficiently if—number of 'readers' assented that it was so?), this plausible explanation, is no more real than the thing-in-itself could ever be.

Narration is what you do as a writer (& human being) vis-à-vis the gapping process ('gaps' being the nouns) you are preoccupied with/in front of you always, that you are convinced makes an order (relation) in which such can be experienced (don't have to), although you are the more Narr for thinking any such thing.

Can 'the way a story is told' in peculiar shape of any extant, particular language one 'writing gentleman' grows up inside & as a child, tossed around, have 'anything to do with' how what we know is happening?

Narrative is how we know what we know is happening. It's not just a 'mental process'—it's what we do (e.g. a wave of the hand), but only as connective tissue recognition/socially studied response & (furthermore) potential group new testament pronounces now what's going on.

What's going on? Asking this question forbidden, just as it would be— this instantly revolutionary inquiry has to be stopped! Relegate it to the Arts, where 'different combinations', 'new ideas' & 'bold realizations' can be expressed safely, ad nauseam—without ever getting into the ring with the 'real', political, story line.

This is more a question that narrating has to answer, nowadays, than anything 'I' knows.

"I'm going upstairs to get . . ." is not presently an answer to anything, nor an account of any sort. Psychology doesn't really answer. So, narration of some kind is necessary.

Kind is nature, children, etc. To stay alive.

Narration is natural process as we know it 'understandingly' in our minds & actions, e.g. as poets, so could verse forms show it today.

Today, seemingly, something else could also be any place—nothing is not only rampant, nihilism could be anywhere. Venture capital says any form shall be.

Important to investigate 'sequence' in order to find out order in which everything seems to be happening, but it isn't—'sequence of events' as we commonly know it in America is a front. It's up to narration to discover the right way night & day happen—not just 'experiment', but actual story—again/anew.

Narration is <u>the</u> moral responsibility for the writer-fool—one has to keep trying to figure out how <u>that</u> took place, in writing—& certainly inscribing <u>numbers</u> on a page has historically been importantly associated with articulating "dogmatic" conditions—be it the conviction that telling something in 1, 3 or 2 pages might accomplish it.

Reading left to right, up to down, establishes a convention that, together with the turning of pages, assumption of 'the speaker'—oh gosh, just too much artifice to deal with, here—all that <u>stuff</u> is taken to be what's happening—what's freezing into a set, 'in our lifetime'. Poetry is . . .

Other ways to try to relate & so know what's happening as a matter of interest, purely for itself (as a kind of 'mission' given by itself to itself to do), are being stamped out. Actual investigation of condition of experience via venturing account of what's happening (a 'relation') discouraged by worldwide spread of 'basic' binary evaluation of everything as 'can do'/'no way'. Stupid.

Much current narrative stupid. <u>Can't be the case</u>.

Narrative is the eye of the diamond, the tool, the measurer, the 'section'.

Gertrude Stein understood the horizon of narrative as <u>both</u> the idiot belief in what was said to be happening customarily ("human nature") <u>and</u> the occurrence of another, knowledgeable presentation of events (the "human mind"), results of which at first look ugly, & then beautiful / 'true'.

It's morning. Finally, Zukofsky's <u>It Was</u>. Ought to heat a can of soup, or listen to music.

Preoccupation with narrative can only yield you what it <u>was</u>?—e.g. that aforesaid, previously ordained feel of <u>plot</u>, in even so 'good' a novel as <u>Bleak House</u>?

The true order of events is both 'composed' and 'given', in a rhetoric which inevitably both 'conceals' & 'reveals'—e.g. Heidegger in translation doesn't really g<u>o</u>? Possibly in the original it does circle. Learn German.

I said I would look up "narrative" to myself.

II

Early verse, after 'learning poems', was preoccupied with series, with speech as series since I had inherited that form, there was really no investigation into narrative going on there, that was the was (sic) the world was (<u>Series</u>) why it was.

Sentences was attempts to stop time, prosodically (see Stein's "Composition as Explanation"), as I knew it—periodically, were, in order to be able to start it up again, to see it—by attending to different specific finite in relation durations & rhythms, as these could be apprehended in words making words ("from rhythm to image") again tolerating each other's differences as different seen & heard differentiations within the 'same' sound world (read time). More than one could be read through twice or more, around loops that aspired less to be more 'short poems' than to go on 'for all time'—'smaller'/'bigger'?—some relief from reiteration produced by a various insistence, absent time (like a slice of which?). Each stood out separately, claiming its own time, thus all was its own time—each had the time of its own.

So narrative became what I was at the time following—then Central African Pygmy music, one Ocora Dahomey record, for example, steered me to hear the separate notes in a mosquito's clustered buzzing & horns as being separate sounds making all big one sound—also different rhythms being tolerated & encouraged inside the same one-big-time that everybody was cognizant of as she played his (lute) solidly different part transparently concentrated in that & regardless of the time of the others, so the better to make those noises—that proves the existence of the possibility of true group consciousness in the music itself—MA!—respecting & encouraging different 'narratives' of which it is built (Jack Kerouac was also important here—e.g. the football pass sequence in his Visions of Cody—& of course also Robert Creeley all along & throughout, but especially in Pieces (parts are wholes/parts of a whole) & Presences, Joanne Kyger in person, Kenneth Irby, Anselm Hollo, Emily Dickinson, Emily Lord, Gertrude Stein, William Carlos Williams, John Keats, Ezra Pound, Walt Whitman, Charles Olson, Larry Eigner & Louis Zukofsky).

Meanwhile, the world was willed to chance, to change, by guaranteeing the separateness, but still finite (at large) <u>possible</u> relations among the communities of the <u>different</u> cards. 'Necessary' alliances shewed to be structurally absurd by apparent <u>abundance</u> of actuality-in-possibility, 'narrative' would be brought to a stop (but be seemingly infinitely <u>jumping</u>) by the (halt) (oxymoron) brought about by the author, arbitrarily, perhaps, but still in the service of—THAT that rules the waves.

It's an exuberant & perhaps 'youthful' aesthetic/athletic delighting in the actualization of <u>any</u> sequence as a 'sentence' that appears to contribute to & record, that that happens—<u>that</u> <u>did</u> <u>happen</u>—over against the myriad things as sequence-structures in language that 'might have been' & 'weren't' for that time, that were evident as articulately clattering nonetheless <u>ghosts of</u> <u>possibility</u> & <u>figures</u> <u>from</u> <u>the</u> <u>past</u>—formal resources vastly more potential, all that 'didn't' or 'hadn't'—were constantly struttering about, as possibles-in-actuality always almost before one's nose?

More force to the democratization of syntax-sequence! Demote the fixed! Totalitarian view of what looks like the 'normal course of things' 'inevitably' nowadays <u>downfall</u> toward depletion of the given planet, <u>begone</u>! Faith in the miracle of the middle structure-world apparently needed/occurring in language, as its process reality (why this one, rather than another one—or nothing—here?)—-that's "narrative" in <u>Sentences</u>.

More Kerouacian occur more recent tirades for & against a lot of things more recently & at length, <u>see</u>, thrash about to move by rhapsody through a sequence of words—

    patient Rhapsody being led to
    the world by a sequence of words

III

These various stories are taking place here, in the forest, whether we presently live in the little blue cottage with Debra, or ever did so, or died, or want to or don't or what, because they <u>are</u> <u>possible</u>—i.e. can happen, because they do happen in a sequence of language particles so hereditary / arranged ('by whom'?) that that becomes an order in which autumn boughs & the like are experienced—<u>shown</u>—by such process as conjunct forces activated / greeted by such process—like a "dumb show of kings"—

kept on going to the corner store

accomplishes <u>that</u>, as if (ill?) <u>fated</u> <u>to</u> <u>exist</u> <u>in</u> <u>that</u> <u>line</u>. Maybe so. But you got to keep in mind the role human cognitive capacities & skulls as perceptual means have in it, as its shaping of it.

Narrative is a means to tell the truth, albeit not all of it has to be presented, for the time, as the whole of it. Every thing told moves, means many things not being told, with it. Everything can't be told all at once / at the same time—hence, narrative. Nothing is necessary & even sometimes apparently appropriative-automatic. <u>Bang-bang</u> could mean the end of you, <u>if</u> "you" already were the 'character' shot.

Narrative has nothing to do with traditional fictional apparatus, <u>except</u> <u>insofar</u> <u>as</u> <u>it</u> <u>happened</u> (<u>it</u> <u>was</u> the story)—plot, characters, metaliterary authorial omniscience, supposed relationships between a 'speaker' & a 'reader' or, & especially, this fiction of the impertinent insistent "tale told by an idiot" who mariners or "stoppeth one of three." <u>Nonsense</u>. Sickening.

Narrative is just the minutiae—all here rhythm / image order in which something occurs, in language, around us—often only the very sequence of the letters themselves. Writing celebrates this order of the syllables—as how something occurs as it is. It might have been otherwise, truly. Bungalow.

Interesting writing contains this possibility of the 'might have been' within its very assertion that something <u>bushy red</u> was happening—"dawn"—every 'is' rests by/presumes a 'was' that was its parent sometime ago anyway, hoary with body, & especially a 'might come to be'—pukes—that births it most importunately in the mind of an author fortunate in being occasionally able to state it in the sequence in which it occurred—e.g. by Kerouac write-fast.

Occurs. But the order of events that <u>does</u> happen in language <u>is</u> significant. (E.g. <u>A Day At The Beach</u>, set of six things on a page where two 'columns' stacked 3-each, everywhichway, maintain a 'story-line' in various directions—'purely the possible'—while maintaining a sturdy 'narrative line' throughout, <u>leaning</u> on the top-to-bottom/left to right 'development' of the 'thrice-told' seventy-two frames. Columns of events, for sure, one says.) Never demean it, for by it your livelihood flourishes. Written or not, the sledgehammer contemplation of things with clumsy orders of verbiage—& <u>printing</u> of same, if that route, impressing paper—is a furious, fortuitous, foolish & noble act. Narrative, for the time, serves as the 'music of the spheres' for a generation of writers convinced & nervously uncertain only about the precise 'timing' & 'panoply of events' at the end of the world?

What if life remains to be discovered? What if language still could be used to wrest 'objects' from 'experience' towards reality in the literal strata of the words? What then would be the purpose of preaching the 'end of the world'—if by your very usage you had abandoned all interest in further <u>life</u> <u>via</u> <u>syntax</u>? As now. And with or without further nuclear happenstance, you were drab, sequentially conventional & markedly conversational? Huh? Why, then, you would have "stopped the world"—at whatever point in the 'argument' you standed.

Some might rival Venice in their power.

Eyes can but shine to recall the honor of being the one told—so it always seems (<u>viz.</u> the moon shining 'for me alone' across the water)—these six different stories by these six different 'authors', each one <u>still</u> trying to impress on me the virtue of—how they must have warred 'for my heart'(?) in the family.

Mother and Father, Helen & Judd, were the narrators in my experience, along with Aunt Ragnhild & Aunt Augusta.

IV

What's the 'connective tissue'? What does "it makes another syntax" mean? 'Syntax' & 'narrative' <u>clearly</u> <u>indicate</u> (?) 'the same thing'? What a charming muddle!—Darling, don't leave!

Almost everything remains to be undertaken in the investigation of 'narrative'—we don't know what it is—what's the 'symbiosis' between language (apparently a 'structural event') & human (animal, generally, huh? semicolon; rocks?) 'mental process'—"language"?/"mind"? ("language area"—'in' the brain?)? Almost everything is "in quotes" including, particularly, that previously casually supposed copy-relation among/between "language" & "the world" (now presupposed to be merely the image, purely projected by men's & women's wills, <u>as</u> <u>language</u>, within which 'we' are trapped, rather unfortunately, but within which we <u>can</u> alter the environment by transferring ownership or employing a competent & highly recommended gardener to reduce traffic noise?—the notion of 'syntax' as some total 'governing' language's pre-programmed 'narrative' of 'events' arrived?)?

What's the 'comparative time'? Eh!? How, then, <u>ever</u> know <u>what</u> <u>follows</u>? One thing <u>after</u> another?—"one one one"—what does that <u>language</u> mean? Form is what it looks like afterward, depending 'from' what happens?— well, then, on same old question, <u>how</u> such? Mark <u>what</u> <u>happens</u>, extant sort!—how 'then'?—<u>how did what happen</u>?—the Past, <u>It Was</u>—outcome of what mysterious 'flesh'. . . ? What made it?—<u>something</u> make it?

"Don't mess with narrative!"—absolute dictum of society which would phase you in, phase you out, 'finally'—assumption of "beginning/middle/ end" & series form through which we are supposed to 'live', <u>so</u> heavy-handed & pervasive it's not even noticed—until you step out, on occasion—with 'narrative' as henchman of this <u>awful</u> mind-control, that spreads abroad, with intent to aggrandize whatever it can push/persuade the world is this way to—the whole thing 'organized'—synchronized/in sequence—in our lifetimes!

V

What is the passage of time to time, that's narrative, what is the order in which 'things happen', in 'language' of course—i.e. in & through lan- guage—but more primarily order of events through man perceived to share that same 'structure' that. . .

<u>All</u> writing is essentially 'narrative'—not only storytelling/prose—but any combination of letters, that moves in time.

You always have to tell the story <u>of</u>.

It does <u>its</u> activity as a major means to salute & acknowledge, recognize & 'define' & manifest itself, I write.

The mere activity of a reader 'reading'—by moving through words &
syllables (at high speed or at a crawl) while thinking almost anything about/
never everything by any means of what the words 'say', in toto—makes a
small (unwritten) 'narrative in itself', for itself.

Essentially, the reader makes the narrative—<u>the writer</u>, <u>as a reader</u>, <u>makes
the narrative</u>?

Ok, then, the <u>issue</u> is the same thing (as if the writer makes the story up,
out of the Imagination)—<u>its glory forth</u>—

VI
(for Tom Clark)

What agency has commissioned the account, & for whom?

'Why bother'??

If "agency" be 'the poet', then whom is he benefiting 'in these years
to come'—certainly not himself. <u>We know his time is short</u>, but who are
"we"?

Who is benefiting?

Any time able to be left at all to look around & begin to move to find out?
What is this that wants this?

"Growth of a Poet's Mind"? To meet—who hears everything said?

But who has <u>time</u>, intelligently, to want this (who?) does not see the gathering social impossibility of living on the planet, around us?

And who could continue to go to work—<u>who wants to know?</u>—given this? Up off the horizon, how is it that the <u>clouds</u> continue to shape these estimable patterns?

<u>Who, huh, who</u>?

VII

Humans 'accept' or 'make up a story' most readily when they no longer (need to) <u>need to notice</u> what's happening 'around them', as an interesting, nay, <u>compelling</u>, 'problem' & circumstance—there way is made for them!—by the uniform of which they seek & hear—therefore all mattresses need investigating (but not the Ed Sanders' type—well, <u>that</u>, too)—this would be 'narrative' as looking into the <u>smallest</u> processes of writing (e.g. letter/number relations, 'syllables' & <u>counting</u>) 'stitching together' the 'results' into an amenable & believable & wholly rhapsodic (if 'ugly'), intelligible, fantastic & true Ode revealing the actual as gift of the possible—way would be 'discovered' by usage 'feeling its way' in practice toward the center of language—which would in sentences reveal itself in the <u>most</u> primary sense as 'made of the same stuff' as 'the world we live in every day'—

Hence, <u>task of narrative</u> (despite all current 'theory'/'evidence' elsewise)—<u>words must be</u> 'somehow' <u>the same things as things</u>.

ROSE APPELLATE PROJECT (ENTWURF)
    for Kathleen Frumkin

yellow rose into the composite fathom of the dark day ah
train whistle breaking prolonged still extant under the walnut tree sky
three 'wardens' Chumash moving 'all such birdlike creatures' show as flying
sunlight tissue 'foot' from forms live on so shapes can do
hand writes as a motion of timeless vast phenomena scoring
wall viz. 'miracle muscle' living distinction credence insect
presence style ye gods eyeballs-eyesight differentiation stance belief
spelling light for hymn to day recast around loved sound phantom
petal vocable apparent rose stride forward bulky from the tomb

SENSATION
or
the book called *book*
1969–72

it is a well-lit afternoon
& the heart with pleasure fills
flowing through town
in warm things
yes what do you know
it's winter again
but the days are well lit
what's more
they're beginning to stay that way longer
that is a fact
& i am moving
through a town
in a fur hat
the third one in my life
or is it only the second?
the expeditionary force will have to check up on that
back there in the previous frames
while i move forward
steadily, stealthily
like a feather
i am a father
bearded & warm
& listen to words coming through
the fur hat off a page
in the finnish language:
"when there's nothing else to do
there's always work to do"
my father said that
in one of his notebooks
& it's true

i walk through a town
& up some steps
& through a door
it closes
now you can't see me anymore
but the lights go on, & you know I'm there
right inside, working out

"touring"

window of room nine
college city motel
northfield minnesota
& a fraction to the weaker side of a winter's heart
"white country"
peter schjeldahl's book
& this is his home town
& white country is what one sees here
& then one sees a matchbook it says
"thank you for stopping"
one has stopped here one feels the light (la lumiere)
moves faster sliding across these acres of snow (la neige)
one worries about the future of bears
in public in one house
this is known as a poetry reading
then one proceeds to drink gallons of cider in public
in another house
this is known as getting crocked
one remembers the cider junkies of somerset england
exceeding pale eyes in exceeding red faces
the weird sheen in the paintings of samuel palmer
back in room nine one's brain scanner flickers & zooms
across these endless heartlands of the heart
(el corazon)
the telephone does not function (no funciona)
after the hour (la hora) of eleven p.m.
back in new york & london back in iowa city

one then goes dark
in the collage city motel
in northfield minnesota

between bouts
i keep in shape
for visitors
from e.g. thibet:
a cock
signifying craving & greed
a snake
signifying wrath & passion
a pig
signifying ignorance & delusion
they just decided to drop in
but i tell them all
gettahellouttahere
the western way

in love we loaf
munching love's loaf
it is a fortunate condition
it is a preoccupied porcupine
going about mother maya's business
on an ardent spring night
taking this deep a breath is ardent
like diving
up up & away
keeping the harp in tune
even here, where we are
amerika, no one knows you
but loafing & loving
upon your mighty body
remnant mind & trembling heart
we may yet escape
"planet x goes kablooey"
"bang bang! wowee! that's neat"
no it ain't, son
except in the most particular way it happens
continually, in your skin
your flesh, your bones, your art
which is what keeps it going, you understand

"art & literature"

let me recommend
the "dennison" series of seals
the twenty-five cent booklet
"cat seals" in particular
it contains a wonderful persian
electric blue fur
& amber eyes
it's a classic!
gerry gilbert has created a classic, too
it's called "phone book"
you order it from weed flower press
seven five six bathurst street toronto canada
a dollar and a half, & you should act now!
the grass sits mumbling under the snow
memorizing its survival techniques
must end this now
there's folks drooping in

long hours one labors at the desk
to come up with these funny
little chunks
lime samson agonistes
all for the birds or anthologists
one has a staggering cold today
but one can read
unlike the unfortunate
eighteen point five million americans
who can't
"the tibetan mysticism of john 'tantric' blofeld"
"wishes lies & dreams"
"american indian lives"
staggering lives
the world loves
"the world anthology"
but no one even likes "british poetry since 1945"
which is just a roomful of music boxes
confidently playing "lara's theme"
but one does like one poem in it
peter pewter's haiku "alone in the kosmos"
it so brief one quotes:
"i kneel by the infinite sands of the stars.
my hat blows off the planet.
dinner is in doubt."

"old space cadet speaking"

let me tell you, the captain knew
exactly what he would do
soon as he reached the destination
he would fuse with her
plumulous essence
& they would become a fine furry plant
later travelers would run their sensors over
to hear it hum
its favorite song
"call me up to dreamland"
by the old minstrel known as "the van"
ultimate consummation of long ethereal affair
he knew he would miss
certain things small addictions
acquired in the colonies
visual images baloney sandwiches
but those would be minor deprivations
hardly bothersome in the vita nuova
he was flying high
he was almost there
& that is where
we leave him to go on hurtling through the great warp
& at our own ineffable goals

at this point, the moon
starts to take on a little brown & gray
as opposed to being so very bright
as it appears from earth
*
up in the andes
an old peruvian
in a featherwork mantle
sits listening to his god
his god is playing looney tunes
on the organ of novelty
while down below in iowa city
a small dane is freaking out in a drugstore
shoving & beating the other customers
yelling this is my drugstore my drugstore
get out get out
the proprietor calls the cops
& they take him out
because it isn't his drugstore
a large unclear device explodes in alaska
furious hurricanes sweep through the banana fields
old man in featherwork mantle
knows the innate beat of all things
he is engaged in expressing unobservable realities
in terms of observable phenomena
a great body
of tender & intimate works
to sleep beside him
later

like a large friendly lioness
who loves me
the old peruvian

apollonius
his mother
walks in a meadow
she lies down on the grass &
goes to sleep
some wild swans
at the end of a long flight
approach her & by their cries
& beating of wings
awaken her
so suddenly
he is born

on christmas day nineteen seventy
a small english girl from hampstead near london
walked several miles in sub-zero weather
to see the children's cartoon show at the hampstead cinema
but when she got there
it was closed!
the manager of this cinema happened to pass by
& he saw the little girl "crying & frozen almost blue"
he asked her why she was crying
she told him & he took out his keys & they went in
& he seated her in the empty stalls
& went into the projection room
& the show was *on*
*

that day he was the fastest man on earth

the performance of the world
can happen only through the energy
put forth in producing it
which is maya—the energy
put forth in producing
the performance of the world

on lake titicaca
era of giant tapirs
she stepped out of her craft
oreana
her skin the deep sheen of gold
with weird webbed feet
& hands embraced the boss tapir
thus we began
who have two breasts like her
& intelligence
& a womb like hers
& a tool like the tapir's
thus softly we sing to her
our large-eared lady of tiahuanaco
who went back to her star

pocket-size water pipe
next to tarot pack with the sun on its cover
flanked by some works
by alfred north whitehead & gregory corso
partly obscured by a green glaze jar full of feathers & pencils
now a hand appears in the aer
it removes first the pipe
then one of the tomes of whitehead
finally a feather
smoke drifts over the scene
it is peaceful, peaceful
though there is faint hum of fellow beings next door
busy constructing bombs or other
wishes, lies & dreams
everybody
must
get
bombed

vibrant mutants of the future,
i love you!
but what can you do with this love
or a twentieth century fossil?
well, anyway
i love you to bring you about
that is what love is all about

across the incredible static of time place language
the air of june sings
& heaving the brick through the plate-glass
the people go crazy
head forward trunk back leg up arm down
indefinable heads in bulky suits
traverse the universe
can you see it going on & on
you minute bug
walking across the back of my hand
your life can be measured in minutes & now
i flick you off
that was one of the most exciting days of your life.

sitting by the door
"making moccasins"
thinking about nothing
the sun is halfways down
at the end of the plain
i am talking to the lake
i am talking to all in the lake
i am not a human being
not only a human being
i am pit river shaman
i am jaime de angulo
i am anselm hollo
dog face
son of maya

after verlaine
right now
it is raining in iowa city
but it ain't rainin in my heart
nor on my head
because my head
it wears a big floppy heart, ha ha
it wears a big floppy heart

drinking some cheap but good wine
after tu fu
two thirty a.m.
using all this potential
not one minute of my life have i wasted
you drunkard poet uncles
i like you a lot
my nephews don't
they tired of the twang
you been puttin out
but here, have some wine!
have a good cry

huginn & muninn
odin's twa corbies in orbit
extended his nervous system throughout
they were named after thought
& memory
they were sensational corbies

"impression du matin" (for ted berrigan & alice notley)

hi, folks!
i sing
the cardio-vascular lotus, out of whom spring
channels to the number of one hundred & one
each of these branching
into a hundred channels
& these again into seventy-two thousand smaller channels
"as hair springs
from man's body
& is withdrawn again"
that was the cardio-vascular lotus speaking.
this is anselm,
on a spring day
on jupiter
*

land here!   everything has been prepared!
*

o thank you, thank you
now let us walk together
past all those kindly, weathered, mossy stone lions
& hear what the high folks on this planet have to say.

september nights
even the mastodons'
incessant farting
sounds muted,
autumnal

walked into grandfather
most literally
suddenly sat in his rocking-chair
had only one thumb
wished I could stay, write his life
the one i never really knew

through two layers of glass
the far end of this restaurant
a man
whose head is
a glob
of light
like anybody's
any body
he is formless form
by means of maya
& all her daughters, assumes
innumerable forms
of which i am one, eating out alone

<u>the discovery of lsd a true story</u>

the dose of a mere
fifty micrograms totally altered
the consciousness of professor albert hofmann
motel soda works intersection
swerve hit geode albert
inadvertently
inhaled it
blast core city ominous rock
spiraling rites of light
inhaled his consciousness
& exhaled
"phew! wow! pow! <u>zat</u> voss somsink!"

black elk speaks
black elk speaks & speaks
earth
heaven
walk away
black elk goes on speaking

(for anne waldman)

little asterisks cheer up the page
but poetry is blood
is dwarfs' drink
dwarfs' drunken ship kvasir
zonked? what
do you mean,
"zonked"?
can't hear you
i'm zonked
& the great god whose name is amplifier
feeds his strong signal into the goddess
whose name is speaker coil
& the quantity of air that is moved is huge
& the pressure of that air is heavy
& the sound is loud sweet lord it is loud
*
later, i go out & look at the sky.
it is one great asterisk.
& there are ships sailing in it
with lights & joyful singing,
the dwarfs' charter flight to earth
a mighty flotilla
come in to land
this giant night

hot moon, & still looking
at you, sideways
on country roads long ago
or a little crosseyed at times
but mostly focused on the continuous & projective field
we compose in our walking & talking dreams
where the lover stands ever
in unintermittent imagination of his belovéd
& electric current gives light
where it meets resistance
sweet resistance, sweet suck & push
suck & push, all we know
ever know as the splendors of paradise

key three, arcana major

here we go,
zapping about in the folds of her gown
of an ample cut & seed-pod design
her hair so bound in radiant energy
all twelve stars in her crown
it is the empress we live in
snug up against her skin
that once did open
to let us pass & be in
the born world

<u>nineteen sixty-five</u>

sunday morning
naked woman, bending over
spitting a milky water jet into the basin
returning the toothbrush clack to the beaker
turning to wipe her mouth
cool body washed now & moving fast
changes, formations
pleasing to me as i sit on the can
smoking a pipe in the sun
comes through the blinds
my "zebra belly" remarked on by the daughter
three years old & well on her way
to that same build
though she can still be held
upon one palm
& she's in session too
on her blue plastic pot & even more
creatively engaged
she's threading wooden beads the while
whatever these two do
is interesting

"dune"

beautiful woman, molecules
same as me
you &
your ass
so at home
in rivers
lakes
the sea
you're a very large vision
i believe
the largest vision i ever had
in the light's heart
at the head
of a legion of shaggy dragons
i salute you

the low black square
is a table
once upon a time
its legs were longer
but i sawed them off
i sawed & i sawed
one of them always shorter
than the other three & so
it got a little too low
in the end
kind visitors breathed
"ah, japanese"
& on the black square
the tile-red cylinder
is a pitcher we found in venice
we were happy there
in a pitcher we found in venice
there are flowers
they are flowers
they're just some flowers

i call your name
clear as joe brainard's prose
a summer's day
wondering where you are
just want you to know i have not forgotten you
since our meeting in toyland
snow starts falling
white as carpaccio's dog watching his master
write some more on the back of the postage stamp
long before the beatles &
i call your name

foghorns on the solent
rumble of rock island line
summer & autumn have passed without you
winter is making ready to occupy this space
vivaldi & coffee
a white man's morning
separated from you, white woman
there is a terrible shortage of you in this house.

double martini

do you remember
i ask the stewardess
how madly in love we were?
when we were four years old
no, she corrects me
not four but fourteen my dear
& here we are
twenty years later & in a dream
her memory seems unimpaired
i kiss her fraternally
then go for a walk round the plane
in the surrounding blue
& through the windows i can still see her smiling
smiling, moving along, serving the lords of this world

"zooming" (for tom raworth)

she looked on him &
the moment she looked
there was no part of her
was not filled with love of him
& he too gazed on her
& the same thought came to him
★
"math, son of mathonwy"
two thousand years of formal design
romance, or: the goodies
we do get off
on those
as the big bird goes thundering through the sky
way up above the humpback whale & his cante jondo
the rose & the sword in one word is weird
"hey, miss
may i have another pitcher of gin?"
★
he placed his hand on her shoulder
& she set off & he along with her
until they came to the door of a large fair chamber
& the maiden opened the chamber
& they came inside & closed the chamber
& no one ever saw them again
but an unceasing flow of wonderful sound poured forth
from that high radio tower
& there's that word now
walks past my window with two humans inside it
as yet unaware of its horrendous designs

the cut-rate shoe store: part of a landscape
otherwise restaurants taxicabs shower curtains
alcohol 'sheer romance'
'hell' & all that
like the more boring
like novelists
now in his sleep he walks past it again
stops stares at hundreds of shoes
all of an equal shoeness
& sees what he was slow to see then
in the vast supermart of i-love-you
where immediately on arrival
he was handed a credit card
*

oh the gods took pity on me
mercifully they kicked my ass
made me come off it before i got hooked
for ever on third-rate third-person movies

"the works"

one
it is fine
two
life is good
three
i would like to make love
four
you are trespassing on my territory
five
she's mine
six
how nice it would be to make love
seven
how nice to have made love
*
those are the works of the male grasshopper
i feel exactly the same way.

my first miss amerika
lopsided face
long legs
big ass
big heart
pleaded for me & cried
all over the senior citizens
who told her they come in all colors
shapes & sizes
but they are devils
& we must kill them

when a poet feels
like a sick owl
he writes
like a sick owl
*
when he was fifteen
sick owl climbed
horse nose butte
& ate some peyote
then he had a vision
he saw this huge owl being sick
all over north dakota
all over the biosphere.

harrison, lennon, mccartney & starr
music on the roof of apple building
let it be
a farewell to civilization as they, & we, have known it

"carolina del norte"

old platinum wool top black face dusty coat ladies
tottering down the road with big shopping
where i see them
half a second of their long time
then "men at work"
road gang
man with shotgun waves me on
one of the men with no shotguns
gives the black power salute
inhumanities over the radio
in the rented plymouth satellite
purring through some fine countryside
further polluting the planet
few billboards
but one with the stars & stripes & the message
"wallace for seventy-two"
"we don't particularly *care* for crazies here"
nobody said it
how come i heard it
me frodo
queasy rider
through schwarzwald nord-karolina night
hail mother of the gods!
wife of starry heaven, whose eye
is on the sparrow
to you it belongs to give means of life
to mortal men
& to take it away

happy the man whom you delight to honor
freely bestow upon me for this my song
substance that cheers the heart
& now i will remember you
& another song also
"remember me
to one who lives there"
twelve hundred miles in this capsule
three jet-hours in another
let me ride easy
all the way back
to where my hands & eyes are upon her

<u>antioch illinois</u>

why are the bronze men chasing hercules?
why does the automobile go grraahhkk! & stop altogether
because things in the sky go kah-boom
because the water hose burst

strange encounter

megalomaniac
midgets
exist
but
uneasily.
yes,
officer.
no,
officer.
my name is
kid sky.
i live in
the elevator.
"you're under arrest."

<u>wall poem</u>

the difficulties are great
the difficulties are not great
the handle keeps falling off
the difficulties are awful

lights, blinking
up at the plane:
masses of greedy
little creatures
like you & me
using up the earth
for drinks at thirty thousand feet
& mines in haiphong harbor
"no quarter!"
& on the ground,
in a well-lit tunnel of sheer desperation
i look to get change for a quarter to make a call
but i don't need it,
here they come, up
two brave co-denizens of hell
to meet me
as if it made sense, &
"hell-o!"
&
"you're thinner"
& yes, i say
yes i am thinner, & my hair's turning gray
& they are deporting me, & there is no way
any of this will ever be made to work again
but it is good to see you

<u>"to be born again"</u>

inside my mother
i make a little fist
& then i punch her
enter another plane
walk right into it
the roaring begins
a few hours later
i stride ashore
"welcome to america"
"th-there's a l-lot of b-bastards out there!"
william carlos williams
one moment please
to adjust machine
two a.m. in bed
says "come on out"
some one in my head
"you've been forgiven"

good morning!
when the big grid
shorts out
it's curtains
curtains
going up
on the new world
where horse-borne man
is an awesome thing

<u>on gopher hill</u>

at times it seems merely a question of how to abdicate
gracefully to those wide-eyed brothers & sisters
who dwell in the earth
but then I am gripped by tender desire
tender desire has me by the balls again
o wide-eyed
human sisters & brothers
it is merely a question of how to abdicate gracefully
to your embraces
& let *them* wait yet a while

the force of being she released in him being
equal to the creation of himself the universe is a place
where he would always want to find her touch
her get lost in the space
ships hailing each other with all the lights on
wires humming & speakers roaring
& a cup of mint tea with honey

cloud of dust or roses (rosé) in the head
of that intelligent monkey face man (rilke)
high on another world
another time
country & western time
earrings horseshoes clear lethal fountains
laughter shaking his mother maya's body & his
as he makes her his mistress
for ever or as close
as you get a book
or drive the big white 'car'
with the black 'interior'
through the exterior & its turning leaves

winter solstice
night & i burn
a handful of pine
needles
holding you in a high
window summer room
blowing my mind
where it belongs
to you, who knows
where to send it
spinning
white body galaxy
gran cairo
& an archer
on the wall
calendar, shooting the last
days arrows in the heart

in the kitchen
at night
florence
& general electric
are large, square, & white.
florence
is quiet.
the general
occasionally hums
a tone-deaf ditty.
they're getting on.
they have their problems,
'malfunctions', & such.
but they're still here, to help us.

rising to the dawn's cold beams
from the plantation of my dreams
i think of all those gone among
the savage peoples & frozen gases
the other side of the sun

(for charles olson)

reading a book
"on growth & form"
to get my head together
& i know it won't grow anymore
the cells are crying & dying
& as to the form well it always was an odd shape
but it's still taping
this book
by d'arcy thompson the dashing biologist
"with the looks of a viking"
& "northern mists"
by carl ortwin sauer
a very clear work
hardly anything else is
i'm tired
of thinking
of things
to say to her
trying not to look at her face
i read "northern mists"
because when I look
it makes me want
to say things & the things
i say
how ever true
are not very clear
it is january
& the world's ill

& the dying of a great being
growth & form
northern mists
& the cave so light so warm
as he reared up
& spread wide his arms

<u>anselm's dreams (for anselm george berrigan)</u>

saint anselm of aosta, le bec & canterbury, a.d. 1033-1109, who spent much of his life attempting to prove the existence of god by logic, "in plain language & by ordinary argument, & in a simple manner of discussion."
*

having heard from his mother, the good ermenberga
that there is one god in heaven above
he imagined, like a boy bred up among mountains
that heaven rested on the mountains
& thus the palace of god was there
& the way up to it was up the mountains
his thoughts ran much upon this

*

& on a certain night he dreamed that he ought to go up to the top of the mountain & hasten to the palace of god, the great king. but before he began to ascend, he saw, in the plain which reached to the foot of the mountain, some women reaping corn, who were the king's maidens but did their work very carelessly.

the boy, grieved at their sloth, & rebuking it, settled in his mind to accuse them before the lord. so having pressed on to the top of the mountain, he came into the palace, & there found the king with only his chief butler for company, for all the household had been sent out to gather the harvest, for it was autumn.

so he went in, & the lord called him, & he drew near & sat at his feet. then the lord asked him with gracious kindness, who he was, whence he came, & what he wanted. he answered according to the truth, & then the lord commanded, & bread of the finest was brought to him by the chief butler, & he ate, & was refreshed before the lord, & plumb forgot to tell him about the careless reapers.

& therefore, in the morn-
ing, when he recalled what he had seen, he believed that he really had been
in heaven, & been refreshed by the lord's bread, & so he declared, before
others.

*

thirty years later, abbot anselm sat apart in a corner of the church, to weep
& pray for his friend.

from heaviness & sorrow he fell asleep & saw certain
highly venerable personages enter the room where osbern had died, & sit
round for judgment.

& while he was wondering what the verdict would be,
osbern himself appeared, like a man just recovering, or pale. three times,
he said, had the serpent risen up against him, but three times he fell back,
& the bearward of the lord, usarius domini, stood by his side & chased the
serpent away.

*

then anselm awoke & knew that his friend was saved, & that the angels do
keep off our foes in the beyond, as the bearwards keep off the bears.

grew up in finland
the south of the land
father philosophos & writer
wrote the works of cervantes in finnish
mother a talker & talker
all over the known world
but really my parents
you were giant white rabbit people
very wealthy & powerful
lived in a palace place
under elephant rock
thrones
robes
& a great golden light
strobed out from behind them

"elephant rock"

the huge weight
& granite shape of it
ten times the size of our house
billionfold growths
over its back & sides
the only country
ever known as the features of god

<u>nineteen thirty-nine</u>

just sit here telling myself all these stories
when the sun is shining
on the granite & the veins in it & the veins
in the back of my father's hand
pine needles moss & the light the light
a great roaring silence
so spacious & hospitable
to the rising voice of my mind

one of the pines has a bend in it
three feet off the ground
the horse's back
about two feet
the neck then stretching straight up
to the sightless head of it
where it becomes so fine
there's no way of telling what goes on there

where was it i
fell asleep in the afternoon
& down
& into a hall
where forceful as ever in her big chair
he who was i there saw her
hum to a thin corner shadow
the brother pale rigid
not a sound then the sister
energy out of a door on the right
but i knew where he lay
went on & entered
the room light & bare
no curtains no books his head on the pillow
hand moving outward
the gesture "be seated"
i started talking, saw myself from the back
leaned forward, talked to his face
intent, bushy browed
eyes straining to see
into mine
"a question i wanted to ask you"
would never know what it was
but stood there & was
so happy to see him
that twenty-sixth day of april
three months after his death

the dimensions of the world

father
& son,
playing dominoes
& "casino"
tonight
as twenty-six years ago.
then, son
goes upstairs,
to bed.
"goodnight,
pardner."
& a good night
to you,
father
out there
in earth, water, fire, air

ORGANISM

EACH BON MOT HAS COST ME A PURSE OF GOLD.
ERASE THE LINES OF THE NIGHT FROM THE COUCH OF THE DAY.
COOL TURQUOISE CRYSTAL FEATHER—WOLF PROTON GYRE.
SCROLLED FERN SHADOW SPORE—BREAST SALT MOON.
Wheel of the galaxy turning in tumbleweed.
Faces of antelope staring from ice cream.
Watches ticking on the backs of turtles.
Tambourines tinkling in apple trees.
Flames full of creatures arising from the mouths of worms.
Bearded men pondering in dreams.
Bees and moths darting on the fields of purple asters.
Odor of hummingbird mint crunched under boot heel.

Maya.

Spirit.

Matter.

River.

Creek.

River.

Matter.

Spirit.

Maya.

Odor of hummingbird mint crunched under boot heel.
Bees and moths darting on the fields of purple asters.
Bearded men pondering in dreams.
Flames full of creatures arising from the mouths of worms.
Tambourines tinkling in apple trees.
Watches ticking on the backs of turtles.
Faces of antelope staring from ice cream.
Wheel of the galaxy turning in tumbleweed.
SCROLLED FERN SHADOW SPORE—BREAST SALT MOON.
COOL TURQUOISE CRYSTAL FEATHER—WOLF PROTON GYRE.
ERASE THE LINES OF THE NIGHT FROM THE COUCH OF THE DAY.
EACH BON MOT HAS COST ME A PURSE OF GOLD.

A PROTEIN MOLECULE IS AN ELECTROMAGNETIC SCULPTURE CHANGING IN TIME.
POETS ARE THE UNACKNOWLEDGED LEGISLATORS OF THE WORLD.
BROW VAIN POLLEN DOLLAR—ROAR FOG SHIT.
VELVET TARTAN CURSE—MILDEW BERRY THUNDER.
White spined bushes on the mountainside caught at sunrise and moondown.
Swift lizards with blue throats rushing past stink beetles.
Music of children singing lost words.
Tails of donkeys hung on walls of a cavern.
Honey flowing over polished marble in fluorescent light.
Catatonic tables spouting fountains of nectar.
Vast deserts of kindness in a ball of cotton.
Gentle fingers touching neck muscles in pain.

Orion.

Taurus.

Pleiades.

Web of liquid galaxies.

Pleiades.

Taurus.

Orion.

Gentle fingers touching neck muscles in pain.
Vast deserts of kindness in a ball of cotton.
Catatonic tables spouting fountains of nectar.
Honey flowing over polished marble in fluorescent light.
Tails of donkeys hung on walls of a cavern.
Music of children singing lost words.
Swift lizards with blue throats rushing past stink beetles.
White spined bushes on the mountainside caught at sunrise and moondown.
VELVET TARTAN CURSE—MILDEW BERRY THUNDER.
BROW VAIN POLLEN DOLLAR—ROAR FOG SHIT.
POETS ARE THE UNACKNOWLEDGED LEGISLATORS OF THE WORLD.
A PROTEIN MOLECULE IS AN ELECTROMAGNETIC SCULPTURE CHANGING IN TIME.

I AM A PARCEL OF VAIN STRIVINGS TIED
BY A CHANCE BOND TOGETHER.
CLOVE PLASTIC SNEER POLLEN MESSIAH FEATHER.
ROSE MORNING LONE BREAD HUNGER.
Helmet and armor streaked with sun in the dark room.
Glitter of morning on rows of rectangular windows.
Naked woman in boots masturbating a horse.
Scream of a dying rabbit.
Breath of a baby on mirrors.
Nasturtiums lying on delicate lace.
Ivory rings set with sapphires.
Smell of black coal in the thicket of junipers.
Holes in quasars.
Aminos.
Rain drops.
Assez eu!
Rain drops.
Aminos.
Holes in quasars.
Smell of black coal in a thicket of junipers.
Ivory rings set with sapphires.
Nasturtiums lying on delicate lace.
Breath of a baby on mirrors.
Scream of a dying rabbit.
Naked woman in boots masturbating a horse.
Glitter of morning on rows of rectangular windows.
Helmet and armor streaked with sun in the dark room.
ROSE MORNING LONE BREAD HUNGER.
CLOVE PLASTIC SNEER POLLEN MESSIAH FEATHER.
I AM A PARCEL OF VAIN STRIVINGS TIED
BY A CHANCE BOND TOGETHER.

THE WORLD OF REASON IS TO BE REGARDED AS A GREAT AND
IMMORTAL BEING, WHO CEASELESSLY WORKS OUT WHAT IS NECESSARY,
AND SO MAKES HIMSELF LORD ALSO OVER WHAT IS ACCIDENTAL.
REVIVE THE PLEISTOCENE!
CURSE MUSK LICHEN SCARF BEARDED RAIN.
FLASHING RHYME TENTACLE SALMON HEART.
Bulky creatures eating the tops of lilac trees.
Peaks in the smog covered with fragile vines.
New spices exploding in the cups of tongue-beings.
Basalt boulders covered with ecru silk.
A yellow feather with a black bar.
Projections of reflected light from the eye-shields of owls.
A gray kitten biting the puppy's stomach.
Dainty wings on the man's head.
Rainbow.
Curves of dots.
Slender line.
Opal.
Slender line.
Curves of dots.
Rainbow.
Dainty wings on the man's head.
A gray kitten biting the puppy's stomach.
Projections of reflected light from the eye-shields of owls.
A yellow feather with a black bar.
Basalt boulders covered with ecru silk.
New spices exploding in the cups of tongue-beings.
Peaks in the smog covered with fragile vines.
Bulky creatures eating the tops of lilac trees.
FLASHING RHYME TENTACLE SALMON HEART.
CURSE MUSK LICHEN SCARF BEARDED RAIN.
REVIVE THE PLEISTOCENE!
THE WORLD OF REASON IS TO BE REGARDED AS A GREAT AND
IMMORTAL BEING, WHO CEASELESSLY WORKS OUT WHAT IS NECESSARY,
AND SO MAKES HIMSELF LORD ALSO OVER WHAT IS ACCIDENTAL.

COMPLEX PROTEINS ARE LIKE SUBMARINES.
NEW SPECIES ARE FORMED WHEN NEW ADAPTATIONS RECEIVE
BETTER LOOP REINFORCEMENT.
BREEZE TRUCK COFFEE CINDER.
NEBULA SPLIT BOOK CURRY KNIFE.
Cries from nowhere making silver snowflakes.
Aluminum towers against pale blue backgrounds.
Dark, soft eyes moving through shapelessness.
Rooms of musk.
Walls covered with pendulous breasts.
A pirate's chest full of the wings of moths.
The cruel, curled laugh of a friend.
Reflections of sparrows in pools of oil.
Cold wax.
Splash.
Claw.
Kiss.
Claw.
Splash.
Cold wax.
Reflections of sparrows in pools of oil.
The cruel, curled laugh of a friend.
A pirate's chest full of the wings of moths.
Walls covered with pendulous breasts.
Rooms of musk.
Dark, soft eyes moving through shapelessness.
Aluminum towers against pale blue backgrounds.
Cries from nowhere making silver snowflakes.
NEBULA SPLIT BOOK CURRY KNIFE.
BREEZE TRUCK COFFEE CINDER.
NEW SPECIES ARE FORMED WHEN NEW ADAPTATIONS RECEIVE
BETTER LOOP REINFORCEMENT.
COMPLEX PROTEINS ARE LIKE SUBMARINES.

CUPID ONCE DID NOT SEE A BEE SLEEPING AMONG ROSES.
THE SATELLITE SURROUND IS THE NEW ARTISTIC MASK WORN BY THE EARTH ITSELF.
HUG SUGAR NOSTRIL WINE.
GYRE CELL PAVEMENT STREAMING MEMORY.
Merry crackle of orange flames in the black pit.
Pine cones hurtling through eternity.
Gingerbread men and scent of cardamom.
The old hen running with the worm.
The octopus burned at the stake.
Thick cream mixed with honey and apricots.
Toy sail boat in the flooding gutter.
An ancient millipede coiled and sleeping.
Grains of serpentine.
Cilia.
Hazelnuts.
Tuft.
Hazelnuts.
Cilia.
Grains of serpentine.
An ancient millipede coiled and sleeping.
Toy sail boat in the flooding gutter.
Thick cream mixed with honey and apricots.
The octopus burned at the stake.
The old hen running with the worm.
Gingerbread men and scent of cardamom.
Pine cones hurtling through eternity.
Merry crackle of orange flames in the black pit.
GYRE CELL PAVEMENT STREAMING MEMORY.
HUG SUGAR NOSTRIL WINE.
THE SATELLITE SURROUND IS THE NEW ARTISTIC MASK WORN BY THE EARTH ITSELF.
CUPID ONCE DID NOT SEE A BEE SLEEPING AMONG ROSES.
THOR   THOR

HUMANITY MUST PERFORCE PREY ON ITSELF LIKE MONSTERS OF THE DEEP.
NO ONE UNDERSTOOD THE PERFUME OF THE DARK MAGNOLIA OF YOUR WOMB.
PRAISE FUR NORTH FACE BOOT HAND.
NEGRESS FREEWAY MUSIC SPIRIT (APRIL) BANNER.
Horns of angels blowing in the growing corn plant.
Pollen streaking down a tube to silent smiling ovaries.
Lumpy plant-beasts side-by-side in mountain rain forests.
Bare feet slapping concrete.
Bombs that flare like psycho dogs.
Mozart sleeping in the closet.
Hailstones rattling on the windows.
Real madonnas clutching putty dolls.
Candles.
Tungsten.
Shins.
Rattlesnake grass.
Shins.
Tungsten.
Candles.
Real madonnas clutching putty dolls.
Hailstones rattling on the windows.
Mozart sleeping in the closet.
Bombs that flare like psycho dogs.
Bare feet slapping concrete.
Lumpy plant-beasts side-by-side in mountain rain forests.
Pollen streaking down a tube to silent smiling ovaries.
Horns of angels blowing in the growing corn plant.
NEGRESS FREEWAY MUSIC SPIRIT (APRIL) BANNER.
PRAISE FUR NORTH FACE BOOT HAND.
NO ONE UNDERSTOOD THE PERFUME OF THE DARK MAGNOLIA OF YOUR WOMB.
HUMANITY MUST PERFORCE PREY ON ITSELF LIKE MONSTERS OF THE DEEP.

NIRVANA ALSO DEPENDS ON THE TREASURES OF THE TATHAGATA.
YET DEATH IS NEVER A WHOLLY WELCOME GUEST.
SWIM MUSIC BARK GLOAMING THUNDER.
LISTENING SMOKE SHEET WRINKLE MORNING.
A blackened face with clouds of blue smoke from the forehead.
Russian wolfhound crunching the ribs of sheep.
An envelope filled with orchid seeds.
Bright green creatures.
Appearance of the Ghost of Love.
Chairs covered with moss.
Palm trees the size of bacteria.
The sexual thrill of darkened autos.
Ammonia.
Ammonites.
Pineapple.
Silver dollars in the stocking.
Pineapple.
Ammonites.
Ammonia.
The sexual thrill of darkened autos.
Palm trees the size of bacteria.
Chairs covered with moss.
Appearance of the Ghost of Love.
Bright green creatures.
An envelope filled with orchid seeds.
Russian wolfhound crunching the ribs of sheep.
A blackened face with clouds of blue smoke from the forehead.
LISTENING SMOKE SHEET WRINKLE MORNING.
SWIM MUSIC BARK GLOAMING THUNDER.
YET DEATH IS NEVER A WHOLLY WELCOME GUEST.
NIRVANA ALSO DEPENDS ON THE TREASURES OF THE TATHAGATA.

THE TOTAL AMOUNT OF GENETIC MATERIAL IN CELLS PROBABLY INCREASED
THEN, AS IT IS KNOWN TO DO TODAY (IN PART AT LEAST) BY GENETIC DUPLICATIONS.
THE SCIENCE OF THE SUFIS AIMS AT DETACHING THE HEART FROM ALL
THAT IS NOT GOD, AND AT GIVING TO IT FOR SOLE OCCUPATION THE
MEDITATION OF THE DIVINE BEING.
TENTACLE CLAW FEATHER SHIT MEAT ROAR.
TRACERY WOLF ROSE HUNGER PRAISE.
Cyclones spinning over glaciers.
Confetti lying on empty beaches.
Antelope skull among ferns.
Children dancing on a cliff in the sunset.
A black dog shitting.
Mouthprint on the window.
Tiny insects carrying pollen.
Skyscraper snapping in the earthquake.
Odor of birds.
Eyebrows.
Fossilized shark tooth.
Rusty fur.
Fossilized shark tooth.
Eyebrows.
Odor of birds.
Skyscraper snapping in the earthquake.
Tiny insects carrying pollen.
Mouthprint on the window.
A black dog shitting.
Children dancing on a cliff in the sunset.
Antelope skull among ferns.
Confetti lying on empty beaches.
Cyclones spinning over glaciers.
TRACERY WOLF ROSE HUNGER PRAISE.
TENTACLE CLAW FEATHER SHIT MEAT ROAR.
THE SCIENCE OF THE SUFIS AIMS AT DETACHING THE HEART FROM ALL
THAT IS NOT GOD, AND AT GIVING TO IT FOR SOLE OCCUPATION THE
MEDITATION OF THE DIVINE BEING.
THE TOTAL AMOUNT OF GENETIC MATERIAL IN CELLS PROBABLY INCREASED
THEN, AS IT IS KNOWN TO DO TODAY (IN PART AT LEAST) BY GENETIC DUPLICATIONS.

CALL TO THE ROBIN REDBREAST AND THE WREN.
I'VE HAD A VISION.
CRUMPLED GOETHE MORNING TURQUOISE.
BLACK CALVES BEAMING SWEAT BREEZE.
Moth the size of a moose head with wings outspread.
Green dye on otter fur.
Sandstone walls studded with levers and buttons.
Steaming oatmeal.
A billion writhing bodies in the shape of a mouth.
A palpable wall of fear and resentment.
Dripping nests of ravens on flowing cliffs.
Fresh Virtues born as arms and legs.
Wet earth.
Meteor.
Harp.
Bronze clasp.
Harp.
Meteor.
Wet earth.
Fresh Virtues born as arms and legs.
Dripping nests of ravens on flowing cliffs.
A palpable wall of fear and resentment.
A billion writhing bodies in the shape of a mouth.
Steaming oatmeal.
Sandstone walls studded with levers and buttons.
Green dye on otter fur.
Moth the size of a moose head with wings outspread.
BLACK CALVES BEAMING SWEAT BREEZE.
CRUMPLED GOETHE MORNING TURQUOISE.
I'VE HAD A VISION.
CALL TO THE ROBIN REDBREAST AND THE WREN.

IT'S THE MYSTERY OF THE HUNT THAT INTRIGUES ME.
PACKED IN MY MIND LIE ALL THE CLOTHES.
INDIGO CHALICE STAR TASTE WRINKLE.
BLOND BOOK CINDER HUNGER BREEZE.
Cracking shells of purple urchins.
Trees in the shape of the smiles of elephants.
Smell of waves on a foggy morning.
Avocados eaten by starving hounds.
The eye of a wolf in starlight.
Children's dreams hidden in pillows.
Interlocking of species to form a being.
The snouted man with violet fur.
Shamrocks.
Copper.
Old bells.
Kansas.
Old bells.
Copper.
Shamrocks.
The snouted man with violet fur.
Interlocking of species to form a being.
Children's dreams hidden in pillows.
The eye of a wolf in starlight.
Avocados eaten by starving hounds.
Smell of waves on a foggy morning.
Trees in the shape of the smiles of elephants.
Cracking shells of purple urchins.
BLOND BOOK CINDER HUNGER BREEZE.
INDIGO CHALICE STAR TASTE WRINKLE.
PACKED IN MY MIND LIE ALL THE CLOTHES.
IT'S THE MYSTERY OF THE HUNT THAT INTRIGUES ME.

THE CURVES OF HISTORY ARE MORE VIVID AND INFORMING
THAN THE DRY CATALOGS OF NAMES AND DATES.
PARTY SPIRIT IS ONE OF THE *PROFOUNDNESSES OF SATAN*.
EARED BREAST KNIFE BERRY NET.
SPIN OCTOBER LOBE FREEWAY ROOF TURQUOISE.
Crystal universe with holes the shapes of diamonds.
Sounds of jackhammers and jets vibrating in cactus meat.
Dragons swimming in water and clinging to pebbles.
Lapis lazuli set in living skulls.
Mummies dancing.
The prayers of coyotes.
Pyramid of horse bodies prickled with spears.
Soups of bird nests and flower stems.
Highways of matter.
Memories of ghosts.
Salt.
Sugar.
Salt.
Memories of ghosts.
Highways of matter.
Soups of bird nests and flower stems.
Pyramid of horse bodies prickled with spears.
The prayers of coyotes.
Mummies dancing.
Lapis lazuli set in living skulls.
Dragons swimming in water and clinging to pebbles.
Sounds of jackhammers and jets vibrating in cactus meat.
Crystal universe with holes the shapes of diamonds.
SPIN OCTOBER LOBE FREEWAY ROOF TURQUOISE.
EARED BREAST KNIFE BERRY NET.
PARTY SPIRIT IS ONE OF THE *PROFOUNDNESSES OF SATAN*.
THE CURVES OF HISTORY ARE MORE VIVID AND INFORMING
THAN THE DRY CATALOGS OF NAMES AND DATES.

TO BE HUMAN REQUIRES THE STUDY OF STRUCTURE.
MAY I NOT AT LEAST SAY, THAT UNLESS I AM RELIEVED
OF THIS CURSED LOAD I SHALL LET WIND?
TIME PEARL TARTAN PEYOTE TASTE.
FLOOD PRAISE WHITE RHYME BERRY.
Fat gods riding burros in the stock exchange.
Slices of pleasure.
Conversations between beds and chairs.
Men in dresses of parrot feathers.
Armored tanks stalled against cliffs.
Beautiful arms in moonlight.
Raspberry sherbet in crystal goblets.
Candied almonds.
Scrolled desks.
Faces of salmon.
The jack of hearts.
Faces of salmon.
Scrolled desks.
Candied almonds.
Raspberry sherbet in crystal goblets.
Beautiful arms in moonlight.
Armored tanks stalled against cliffs.
Men in dresses of parrot feathers.
Conversations between beds and chairs.
Slices of pleasure.
Fat gods riding burros in the stock exchange.
FLOOD PRAISE WHITE RHYME BERRY.
TIME PEARL TARTAN PEYOTE TASTE.
MAY I NOT AT LEAST SAY, THAT UNLESS I AM RELIEVED
OF THIS CURSED LOAD I SHALL LET WIND?
TO BE HUMAN REQUIRES THE STUDY OF STRUCTURE.

IN TRUTH, WE ARE NOTHING BUT MOLDED RIVERS.
LET YOUR EMOTION INTO YOUR HANDS.
BLOUSE HEART CRYSTAL FEATHER MUSK FAT.
ROSE CALVES WRINKLE BLACK RAIN PILLOW.
Speckled falcons gliding through tunnels.
Crowns of expanding meat–thought over pitchers of milk.
Tiny antlers on walnuts.
Collision of shrieking fire engines.
The smell of soot in basements.
Fog slipping over coastal mountains.
The breath of hot bread.
Gigantic shadows of nasturtiums.
A pillar of books.
Real dreams.
Ocean of ink.
Profile of rodents.
Ocean of ink.
Real dreams.
A pillar of books.
Gigantic shadows of nasturtiums.
The breath of hot bread.
Fog slipping over coastal mountains.
The smell of soot in basements.
Collision of shrieking fire engines.
Tiny antlers on walnuts.
Crowns of expanding meat–thought over pitchers of milk.
Speckled falcons gliding through tunnels.
ROSE CALVES WRINKLE BLACK RAIN PILLOW.
BLOUSE HEART CRYSTAL FEATHER MUSK FAT.
LET YOUR EMOTION INTO YOUR HANDS.
IN TRUTH, WE ARE NOTHING BUT MOLDED RIVERS.

·

ABSORB ALL BEAUTIFUL SYSTEMS
TO HEIGHTEN SYSTEMLESSNESS

A CURRICULUM OF THE SOUL
(a multi-genre collaborative text in 28 books) is derived from "A Plan for a
Curriculum of the Soul" written by Charles Olson. John Clarke, who both
selected and assigned the subjects, served as general editor for the project
until his death in 1992. Since then Albert Glover has continued this work
and is solely responsible for the final editing of the text.
Thanks to Victor Coleman, proofreader.

The authors, in order of appearance, are

Volume One
Albert Glover; Duncan McNaughton; John Wieners; Michael Boughn;
Lisa Jarnot; Fred Wah; John Clarke; Robert Duncan; Alice Notley;
Robin Blaser; Robert Dalke (editor and translator); George F. Butterick;
Edward Kissam; Edgar Billowitz.

Volume Two
Harvey Brown; Lewis MacAdams, Jr; Ed Sanders; Michael Bylebyl;
David Tirrell; Danny Zimmerman; Drummond Hadley;
James Koller; Gerrit Lansing; Joanne Kyger; Robert Grenier;
John Thorpe; Anselm Hollo; and Michael McClure.

ACKNOWLEDGEMENTS:

I thank the State University of New York at Buffalo which, between 1963 and 1965, created an unusual opportunity for young poets from England, Canada, and the United States to study with Charles Olson and pursue graduate work related to Olson's writing and thought. Professor Albert Cook was especially instrumental in that regard. St. Lawrence University, initially through a grant from the Ford Foundation and subsequently through faculty development stipends to me, supported, in part, the publication of the twenty-eight fascicles that make up the body of this text. Frank P. Piskor, George W. Gibson, Bruce Weiner, and Mark McMurray encouraged this work in various ways. Theresa O'Reilly helped move the project through several generations of computer technology. Guy Berard provided graphic designs for the fascicles and, among other things, taught me how to operate a mimeograph machine. St. Lawrence students Ian Clarke, Michael Sullivan, Tom French, Shirley Webb, Bibi Caspari and Jean Deland provided help with necessary tasks. Mark Jones and his wife Anne devoted two years to keeping the print shop warm and functioning.

From the beginning our project received financial support from subscribers, both individual and institutional, as well as bookstores and booksellers who retailed small press publications. We thank them all deeply since they helped make the project sustainable over three decades. David Abel (The Bridge Bookshop), Kim Andrews, Leslie Arakelian, Ballen Booksellers International, T. J. Bata Library, Joyce Benson, Bob Best, John Bettinger, Robert Bowen, Sheila Bowler, Bowling Green State University Library, Bridwell Library, Brown University Library, Fritz Brune, Don Carli, Douglas Carroll, Alan Casline, Sarah Catchpole, Gary Chriss, Bill Christ, Cody's Books, Compendium Bookshop, Seamus Cooney, Cornell University Library, Cranium Press, Sky Dannneskiold, Prisicilla L. Dawes, Rafael DeGruttola, Chris DiTomasso, Rick Duckles, Eigth Street Bookshop, Theodore Enslin, Clayton Eshelman, Paula Estey, Lawrence Ferlinghetti (City Lights Bookshop), Friends of the Owen D. Young Library, Gregor Gibson, Gotham Book Mart, John Graywood, Green Library at Stanford University, Charlie Greene, Roy Greenspan, Joanna Griffin, Jon Halper, Steven Halpern, Harvard College Library, Michael Heming, Hillman Library at the University of Pittsburgh, Emily Hill, Stillman Hilton at Sawyer Free Library, Dr. Stanley Holberg, Homer Babbidge Library, Scott Hoskins, Peter B. Howard (Serendipity Books), Jamie Hutchinson, University of Iowa Library, Dan Jenkins, Wallace S. Jones, Debbie Williams Keith, Cynthia Kellogg, Peggy Kelley, Kent State University Library, Nick Kimberly, Tom Kinter, Susan Knap, Jennifer Knapp, Susan Knutson, Barry LaBar, Richard Lamb, Gary Lawless (Gulf of Maine Books), Roy Leighton, Herb Levy, Ed Lisbe, Lockwood Memorial Library, Bruce Loder, Jim Lowell (Asphodel Bookshop), Liz MacKenzie, Stechert MacMillan Inc., David MacPhee, Malaspina College Library, Kirby Malone, D. L. Mansell, Marianne Margolis, Ralph Maud, Metropolitan Toronto Reference Library, Roseanne Merry, Tom McGauley, Bruce McGaw, Peter McLaughlin, Gladys McLeod, James Mele, University of Michigan Library, Bruce Miller, New York Public Library, Scott Nicolay, John Nomland, Peace Eye Books, Victor Pease, Stephen Petroff, Cory Porter, Don Powell, James Ramholz,, Bob Randolph, Louis Ray, Bill Reed, Joseph Regenstein Library, David Robinson, Julia Rodgers (Viking Press), Kirk Ruggles, Michael

Rumaker, San Francisco Public Library, Sand Dollar, C. D. Schub, Selkirk College Library, Shaman Drum Bookshop, Pam Schillig, Ed Sharlet, Charles Shively, Simon Fraser University Library, Darrel Simmons, Small Press Distribution, Charles Smith, Lloyd Sokolow, Nina Sola, Louisa Solano (the Grolier Bookshop), Temple Bar Bookshop, Thomas Stender, Bernard Stone (Turret Bookshop), Richard Sturm, Terry Sylvester, University of Texas Library, David Thompson, Bob Tourville, Robert Trammell, Eric van Laer, Phillip Van Voorhis, Eliot Weinberger, James R. Westmoreland, Bill White, Derryll White, Charles Whittingham, David Wilk, Thomas C. Will, Gil Williams, Maxine Williams, Robert Wilson (Phoenix Bookshop), Peter Wyckoff, Jerry Yudelson, and Peter Zachara.

Others who supported this work include: Donald Allen, Barry Alpert, Peter Anastas, Bruce Andrews, Anonym Press, Roger Bailey, Amiri Baraka, Mike Basinski, Franco Beltrametti, Ted Berrigan, Robert Bertholf, Harvey Bialey, Douglas Blazek, Charles Boer, George Bowering, Stan Brakhage, David Bromige, Burning Deck Books, Donald Byrd, Douglas Calhoun, Ron Caplan, Hayden Carruth, Tom Clark, Steve Clay, Victor Coleman, Tim Cook, Robert Creeley, Andrew Crozier, Paul Davison, Diane Di Prima, Peter Downsbrough, Kevin Doyle, Stephen Ellis, Larry Fagin, Brian Fawcett, Vincent Ferrini, Joe Flaherty, Ruth Fox, Diana Gay, Reginald Gibbons, Gerry Gilbert, Allen Ginsberg, Richard Grossinger, Michael Hamburger, George Hitchcock, Robert Hogg, Bob Holman & Elizabeth Murray, Lita Hornick, Andrew Hoyem, Kenneth Irby, William Katz, Karen Kelley, Robert Kelly, Maurice Kenny, Michael Kohler, James Laughlin, Bill Little, Martin MacClain, Nathaniel Mackey, Tom Marshall, John Martin, Howard McCord, Joseph Mehling, John Moritz, Eric Mottram, Anne Noonan, Mark Nunnelee, Joel Oppenheimer, Susan Orlofsky, Bill Ott, Charlie Palau, Stan Persky, Randy Prus, Jeremy Prynne, Jean Radoslovich, Tom Raworth, Peter Riley, William J. Scharf, Kate Selover, Jack Shoemaker, Ron Silliman, Small Press Center, Gary Snyder, Sue Snyder, Andre Spears, Bill Sylvester, John Taggert, Nathaniel Tarn, Tod Thilleman, Anne Waldman, Kenneth Warren, Dutch Wehage, Jonathan Williams, and Karl Young.

No doubt Jack Clarke would have added names to this list. I can only trust you know who you are.

Finally, deepest thanks to B. Cass Clarke and Pat Glover who never doubted our work despite the demands it made upon them.

ROOTS & BRANCHES SERIES TITLES ARE MADE POSSIBLE
IN PART THROUGH THE GENEROUS CONTRIBUTIONS OF

Thaddeus Rutkowski
Lynzee
Lori J. Anderson-Moseman
Richard Martin
Lee Slonimsky
Elayna Browne
Kenneth B. Nemcosky
Barbara Henning
Katy Masuga
James A. Reiss
Elizabeth J. Coleman
K. Feather Hastings
Susan Lewis
Michael Boughn
Karen Gunderson
William Luvaas
Stephen Sartarelli
Gordon Osing
Maximilian W. Valerio
Andrea Scrima
Lewis Warsh
Vitaly Chernetsky
Kathy Conde
j/j hastain
Andrew K Peterson
Marc Estrin
Gloria Frym
Marc Vincenz
Michael Forstrom

Made in the USA
Middletown, DE
15 October 2023